THE GLOBAL COMMONS:
Policy for the Planet

■ ■ ■

By Harlan Cleveland

■ ■ ■

With papers by
Murray Gell-Mann
and Shirley Hufstedler

This booklet is based on a
40th Anniversary Symposium
convened by The Aspen Institute
in Aspen, Colorado, July 5–7, 1989

Published by
The Aspen Institute
and
University Press of America, Inc.

University Press of America®, Inc.

4720 Boston Way
Lanham, MD 20706

3 Henrietta Street
London WC2E 8LU England

Library of Congress Cataloging-in-Publication Data

Cleveland, Harlan.
The global commons : policy for the planet / by Harlan Cleveland :
with papers by Murray Gell-Mann and Shirley Hufstedler.
p.   cm.
"This booklet is based on a 40th anniversary symposium convened by
The Aspen Institute in Aspen, Colorado, July 5-7, 1989."
Includes bibliographical references.
1. Environmental policy–Congresses.   I. Aspen Institute.   II. Title.
HC79.E5C59   1990   363.7—dc20   90–12306 CIP

ISBN 0–8191–7835-7 (University Press of America : alk. paper)
ISBN 0-8191-7836-5 (University Press of America : pbk. : alk. paper)

 The paper used in this publication meets the minimum requirements of
American National Standard for Information Sciences—Permanence
of Paper for Printed Library Materials, ANSI Z39.48–1984.

For Walter Orr Roberts

Scientist and statesman

Leading exemplar of the wider view

CONTENTS

I own one share of the corporate earth,
and I am uneasy about the management.

E. B. White

FOREWORD

In July of 1989, as the first event leading up to its 40th Anniversary in 1990, The Aspen Institute convened in Aspen, Colorado, a symposium on The Global Commons. The program was developed by two Aspen Institute Fellows, Walter Orr Roberts, president emeritus of the University Corporation for Atmospheric Research in Boulder, Colorado, and Harlan Cleveland, former dean and now professor emeritus of the University of Minnesota's Hubert H. Humphrey Institute of Public Affairs. The symposium was organized by Christopher Makins, vice president of The Aspen Institute.

We asked Harlan Cleveland, political scientist and longtime public executive, to capture the rich and stimulating discussion in an essay that would go beyond the bounds of the usual conference proceedings. For this task he had available a full transcript of what was said and by whom, but he was also able to draw upon a lifetime of study and experience in world politics, international economics, and science policy. The concept paper for the symposium was a pamphlet on THE GLOBAL COMMONS, edited by Mr. Cleveland and published by the Humphrey Institute in 1988 as part of its policy research effort called "Rethinking International Governance."

The purpose of the symposium was to consider (in a context that illustrates The Aspen Institute's four decades of contributions to public policy and executive thinking) an emerging concept of potentially great power—metaphorical power at first, but also, as time goes on, a practical influence on national economic and social priorities, the strategies of international business, and the governance of our global environments.

That emerging concept is this: For important parts of the human environment—the physical environment (the atmosphere, outer space, the oceans, Antarctica) and also for the preservation of genetic diversity and the management of the global flow of information—it may be best to think of the world as a commons and to manage some of its key resources in common.

The leading edge of this global change of mind is the converging scientific consensus on, and the growing public awareness of, the prospective global warming produced by the "greenhouse effect" of civilization's emissions of carbon dioxide and other gases. This issue was considered in the Aspen symposium, but in a wider-than-usual context that treats it as one of several upcoming issues in The Global Commons.

Special thanks are due to Walter Orr Roberts, who first proposed the topic and (with Harlan Cleveland) served as co-chairman of the symposium. A scientist of the sun and the atmosphere, Walt Roberts became one of the world's premier science statesmen. He has served for many years as a trustee of The Aspen Institute and one of its foremost inspirations.

For one session, we persuaded two of this nation's outstanding thinkers to address themselves to an idea new to them: that the world's information flow might also be viewed as a kind of commons. The symposium comments of Shirley Hufstedler, lawyer, former federal judge, and the first U.S. Secretary of Education, and Murray Gell-Mann, Nobel laureate in theoretical physics and Renaissance man in many other fields, seemed to the author of this booklet so wise and imaginative that he secured their permission to reproduce them in full, in the final two chapters. Together with some of Mr. Cleveland's comments, they were also published in the second issue (January 1990) of our new journal, THE ASPEN QUARTERLY, edited by Sidney Hyman.

David T. McLaughlin
President
The Aspen Institute

THE GLOBAL COMMONS

What is at stake in all of this is the fate of the global commons. We are all dependent on maintaining the habitability of the planet. We are approaching the time when there will need to be some form of international management of these global commons. That is the quintessential challenge for mankind in the next century.

Robert M. White

PART ONE

■ ■ ■

The Physical and Biological Commons

1

CONCEPT OF THE COMMONS

Do you remember the good ship Mobro? It was the New York barge that took a 6,000 mile voyage with 3,100 tons of garbage, and was turned away by six states and three nations. Its malodorous cargo eventually found surcease in a Brooklyn incinerator. Altogether a lovely metaphor for some of our self-generated troubles. It got a big laugh around the world. (Cartoon wife to husband: "Do you realize that our garbage had a longer cruise than we did?")

The week the Mobro achieved international fame, I happened to be in Paris exploring the concept of The Global Commons with an international group assembled to rethink international governance—or as we put it, "to do postwar planning without having the war first." (We were in Paris because one of our collaborators, the Charles E. Lindbergh Fund, was celebrating, in May 1987, the 60th anniversary of The Flight.) Our focus was on what we could learn from experience in the oceans about how to manage the exploration and use of outer space.

Of course the garbage barge came up in our seminar. At least in outer space, someone said, there would be plenty of room for garbage. Not so, said astronaut Ed Mitchell, who commanded one of the Apollo missions to the Moon. "If there were only one gram of debris per cubic kilometer, out to a thousand kilometers from Earth, the average useful life of a satellite orbiting in that space would be no more than seven hours."

There was a moment of shocked silence. Then someone spoke up: "So we urgently need a space sanitation program?" Sure, said Ed Mitchell. "But remember that a vacuum cleaner won't work in a vacuum." By then, it was clear to all of us that we had better prevent the damage, not just try to clean up after it happens.

3

■ ■ ■

Both to prevent damage and enhance the global environment, it should be useful to think about our surroundings as if its parts were related to each other. Because they are.

That was the premise of The Aspen Institute's international symposium on The Global Commons, held in Aspen, Colorado, from July 5 to 7, 1989, beginning a year-long celebration of the 40 years since Walter Paepcke assembled some of the world's heaviest thinkers, including Albert Schweitzer and Mortimer Adler, and established The Aspen Institute, in a ghost town left over from silver-mining days, as a center for executive education and what its longtime president Joseph Slater called "thought leading to action."

By July 1989 even governments had noticed the close connections between the global environment and international governance. The political leaders of the seven leading democracies had just met in Paris, feasted on the best French food, got caught in a legendary traffic jam at the Etoile, but found time to talk about what we, the world's people, are doing to the only livable biosphere we have. Their communique spoke of "serious threats to the atmosphere . . . the growing pollution of air, lakes, rivers, oceans and seas; acid rain; dangerous substances; and the rapid desertification and deforestation. . . ."

Four enormous environments, still mostly unexplored, are treated in international law and custom as parts of a global commons. Outer space, the atmosphere, the oceans, and Antarctica are geophysically and biochemically related to one another— and cousins also in the human psyche. But each has its own human relations history.

The oceans have the longest human history. Because they were accessible only to a few intrepid seafarers but a dangerous mystery to most land-dwellers, the oceans have long been an unregulated highway for those with the technological prowess to travel it.

The most recent Law of the Sea Treaty declares the deep ocean and its seabed to be a commons. The Holy See spoke in 1978 of the "universally accepted" principle that the seas are "the common

4

heritage of mankind"; the Pope's thinkers neglected to explain from whom mankind received the inheritance. Under the treaty, large chunks of ocean space out to 200 miles from the world's shorelines are reserved as exclusive economic zones, to be managed by the nation-states that happen to be nearby. But even in these zones, the resources are held by the shoreline states in trust for the generality of humankind.

As useful marine resources have been discovered and per-ceived to be scarce, nations have tried to make up rules for their exploitation. The difficulty of regulation increases with distance from the shore (offshore oil, seabed minerals) and mobility of the resource (fish). The United States Congress got into very deep water indeed when it tried to establish the principle that a salmon spawned in a Pacific Coast river would remain an American citizen throughout its life as it traveled the open seas before returning to its ancestral home.

Outer space and its celestial bodies were declared to be the "common province of mankind," in the Outer Space Treaty of 1967. The concept assumed that exploration outward from Earth will be unique, establishing a kind of monopoly on which human decisions will be dispositive.

(Human decisions are notoriously undependable. Two years later, I watched in disbelief as humankind's first envoys drove a large American flag into the lunar dust. Planting the national flag has always been a symbol for conquest, a sign that citizens are claiming real estate for their sovereign. What was NASA up to? A friend tried to relieve my misery at what should have been a moment of triumph. "NASA doesn't really *mean* it," she explained. "This is just for television." She was right: The United States never did stake a claim to the lunar Sea of Tranquility, that perfect metaphor for peace on Earth.)

Since then, the exploration of the heavens has produced a good many high-tech spectaculars, from man-in-space to televised photos of our solar system's outermost planets. But using space to improve conditions for human life on Earth has been the most important result of the space programs so far. Along with whatever farther-out space missions are in our horoscope, the biggest investment will probably be in launching the kinds of machines and types of people likely to be most useful for studying, managing, and peacekeeping down here where most of us are going to be living, working, and maybe fighting in the centuries to come.

Weather and climate ("climate" is long-term weather) have likewise not been claimed as the exclusive province of any nation. Clouds, winds, and storms, unlike human artifacts such as aircraft, move through "national air space" without picking up any of the attributes of national sovereignty.

Atmospheric pollution is obviously everybody's business. It is generating international conflict (acid rain), concern (global warming), and cooperation. The 1987 Montreal Treaty, to avert further damage to the ozone layer, was signed by 46 nations and at the beginning of 1989 had been ratified by 31 of them. "We strongly advocate common efforts," said the seven Paris summiteers in July 1989, "to limit carbon dioxide and other greenhouse gases, which threaten to induce climate change, endangering the environment and the economy. . . ."

An outstanding example of cooperation, so successful you never hear about it, is the World Weather Watch. This is the global system for data collection and analysis, coordinated by the World Meteorological Organization. It makes possible the five-day forecasts by which we all live and work, complete with those time-lapse satellite photos of cloud cover that we see every evening on TV.

Antarctica was established as a special kind of commons when in 1959 a dozen nations, most of which had laid claim to pie-shaped slices of the empty continent, signed the Antarctic Treaty. A few others have since joined the still-exclusive club. Ten years ago, before the Gorbachev era, a Soviet delegate thus described the Antarctic arrangements: "For the first time in history, a whole continent was declared a zone of peace and international cooperation."

A unique feature of the Antarctic Treaty is that it does not provide for an organization, not even a secretariat; there are simply periodic meetings of the signatories in one or another of their capitals. Any nation with the technical capacity can conduct scientific research—or just explore, as Will Steger and his international team are doing by dog sled—anywhere on the icy continent.

Military operations are not allowed and nuclear weapons are banned. You don't need a visa to visit Antarctica, but you do need lots of help to get there and survive.

The treaty comes up for review in 1991. It doesn't have to be reviewed, but it may face challenges both from jealous outsiders hedging against the discovery of minerals under the ice or just offshore, and from insiders (Argentina? Chile?) that still hanker after a slice of the frozen pie.

■ ■ ■

These four environments are very different from each other. Yet there are striking similarities; I am especially impressed with four of them.

First. They are for practical purposes indivisible. They are bounded by each other. They affect each other's behavior. They must take each other into account.

Indeed, it is sometimes difficult to tell where one of them begins and the other leaves off. When I worked in the State Department, I chaired an interdepartmental meeting convened to decide where the "atmosphere" stopped and "outer space" began. You can imagine the argument: the Air Force wanted the boundary to be as high as possible, the space people wanted it much nearer Earth; even the emptiest environments can generate "turf" disputes. After a long discussion my colleague Tom Wilson handed me a note: "Is it necessary to answer this question in order to have a Space Program?" I read this commonsense query to the group, and a thoughtful silence followed. No one could think of a practical reason for establishing a precise boundary between air and space. The question has not been authoritatively answered to this day.

Second. No person, corporation, or nation can establish exclusive ownership of the oceans, outer space, the atmosphere, or Antarctica. But it is possible for a person, corporation, or nation to try to control some of the resources these environments may contain—not information, at least not for long, but such physical resources and properties as fish, krill, oil, hard minerals, energy vents, upwelling cold water, induced rain, the electromagnetic spectrum, gravity-free manufacturing, solar energy, hydrogen, and other useful elements. But to establish and hang onto rights to use the Commons depends on the acquiescence of those who care, supported by the apathy of those who don't.

Third. The four environments that we have grouped as the Global Commons are by their nature sharing environments. That means that transactions in the Commons will tend to be, have to be, sharing transactions, not "exchange" transactions.

The legal framework for international politics, trade, and finance is solidly based on who owns what. The Commons environment belong to no one—or to everyone at once, which is for practical purposes the same thing. What cannot be owned exclusively cannot be bought, sold, given or seized. It has to be shared. For sharing environments we do not yet have either a solid body of law or a settled theory of political economy.

Fourth. For all these reasons, widespread international cooperation is required to explore these environments and exploit their usable resources. Hence the elaborate arrangements, worked out through the International Telecommunications Union, to divide the frequency spectrum by nations and purposes. Hence the Law of the Sea, the Antarctic Treaty, the Outer Space treaties, and the current debate about international public law for the atmosphere. Several speakers at the Aspen symposium stressed the need for fairness, the need to make sure that access to and benefits from the Global Commons are not available only to the technologically strong.

The Law of the Sea Treaty is the most comprehensive legal regime ever devised—and it represents only the beginning of the cooperation that will be needed to avoid further conflict and enhance cooperation in the management of the world's marine and seabed resources. The microcosm of Antarctic cooperation is equally fragile, with the Treaty so soon coming up for review.

The global weather is already under daily surveillance in a coordinated system involving most of the world's sovereignties. Study of the global climate has already been successfully undertaken by some of the most far-reaching international research work in human history. There is also a U.N. convention on induced environmental change. But as the sciences and technologies create

8

the capacity to modify the weather at human command, new concepts of law and practice will have to be invented to match humankind's new power to change its physical surround. Already our *inadvertent* modifications of weather and climate, with consequences such as smog, acid rain, ozone destruction and global warming, present challenging puzzles for scholars and decision-makers alike.

In outer space, international cooperation has so far been achieved in tiny steps—the Apollo-Soyuz mission, agreements about the treatment of astronauts or machines that land in unintended places, and space travel by a few persons and scientific experiments not originating in the nations with launch capabilities. And those steps have been overshadowed in recent years by the prospect of military rivalry in this newly accessible environment. Yet a national commission, in its report to the President of the United States ("Pioneering the Space Frontier," 1986), saw no alternative to cooperative behavior: "Exploring the Universe is neither one nation's issue, nor relevant only to our time. Accordingly, Americans must work with other nations in a manner consistent with our Constitution, national security, and international agreements."

2

AWARENESS OF THE COMMONS

With jarring suddenness, millions of people in dozens of countries are becoming aware of global changes that are liable to affect them personally. For, as Tom Wilson once put it, "Some time in recent years, the works of humans began to outweigh the works of nature in the global scheme of things."

What people do half a world away—chop down their tropical forests, leach their soils, burn oil and coal, blow toxic wastes out of smokestacks and exhaust pipes, pollute the oceans, buy and sell narcotics, engage in indiscriminate sex, have too many babies—is now relayed through sensitive and complex webs of atmospheric chemistry, ocean currents, market trends, and human communication to our very doorsteps, yours and mine.

And what "we" do, we in the more affluent parts of the world, affects people worldwide more than what "they," in the world's "developing" economies, do—because, except for making babies, we do more of all these things than they do.

Self-proclaimed environmentalists and "Greens" have been a fringe element of public debate in industrial countries for a generation. But during that generation, they have become increasingly influential. "As crude a weapon as the caveman's club, the chemical barrage has been hurled against the fabric of life," Rachel Carson wrote in 1962—and her *Silent Spring* was a best-seller, one indication among many that people-in-general usually catch onto fundamental trends before their political leaders do.

In the 1970s *The Limits to Growth*, an early computer projection by an M.I.T. group for the Club of Rome, suggested that the way things were going, we would soon run out of key natural resources. The book sold 3,000,000 copies in multiple languages.

Exponential forecasts of global population suggested that the numbers of people depending on this dwindling resource base would create Malthusian policy dilemmas; "life boat" and "triage" came to be popular metaphors among scholars of world resources. Changes in ocean temperature (especially the *El Niño* effect off the western coast of South America) and drought in the Sahel were widely discussed as somehow related to each other; the argument of one Mexican scholar, that it was not drought but structural discrimination against the poor that killed most of the victims of drought in Africa, was probably true, but most people preferred to blame the weather.

In the 1980s, the pileup of environmental issues promoted them from the professional literature to front-page news. Air pollution in some of the world's great cities, international controversies about acid rain, the crawling expansion of deserts, the destruction of rain forests, the ozone hole over Antarctica, oil spills, the decimation of humpback whales, and above all the idea that the globe might warm up at rates portending disaster for much of humanity, caught the public attention. Once the province of the soberer editorial pages, these now-familiar "problems" made their way onto TV and radio newscasts and the covers of newsmagazines: *Newsweek* featured the threat of global warming and *Time*, abandoning its generation-long tradition of picturing well-known heroes and villains on its first-of-the-year cover, named the whole earth as 1988 Planet of the Year.

In the spirit of our branches-and-twigs mode of learning, we have studied the parts of our global environment in different disciplines, read and heard about them in separate stories, allocated them to specialized agencies (and "czars")—and acted on them with less-than-global perspective.

Would it be useful, for a change, to think about them all at once—especially since new techniques of observation (such as orbiting satellites) and of simulation (by the use of supercomputers) provide an abundance of raw material for more comprehensive thinking?

■ ■ ■

The newly recognized physical circumstances, compounded by the new awareness, have together created a new class of problems, requiring unprecedented kinds of solutions. Two assertions can be made about these fundamentally similar problems:

They are global. They require people everywhere to widen to world scale what they worry about and try to do something about.

Dean Abrahamson, scientist and environmentalist at the University of Minnesota's Hubert H. Humphrey Institute of Public Affairs, has a graphic way of saying this: "When my grandfather was born, environmental concerns were almost all based on housekeeping and trash in the backyard. By the time I was born there were demonstrable regional impacts. The birth of my children coincided with entire river systems and airsheds being affected. Now . . . major global systems, upon which society depends for its welfare, are being destroyed."

They are behavioral. Global change is produced by what we (humanity) have been doing. Its pace and direction can be changed by what we do, or stop doing, next.

Back in the 1970s there was a popular notion that we were running out of key resources. As things turned out, those "limits to growth" were much exaggerated. But meanwhile the evidence has grown that the world's real physical limit may be the capacity of its big garbage dumps (vacant lands and caves, the atmosphere, oceans, and outer space) to assimilate the global output of waste.

The earlier perception shifted as many of us, millions of us, modified our attitudes toward growth, to include not just *more* but also *better*—and decided to protect the environment, too. The newer perception will also shift, as with increasing knowledge we redefine "waste" and use or recycle more of it.

That returns us to the question of human behavior: what we do or stop doing. The key to these global/behavioral problems will be people's willingness to change individual or organizational behavior because of heightened awareness—of population growth, global warming, depletion of tropical forests, acid rain, the spread of AIDS, ocean pollution, famines, natural disasters, the swelling numbers of refugees, the universal trade in narcotics.

As many people change their behavior, they also (usually with some delay) change the minds—or at least the policies—of their political leaders.

This naturally happens most rapidly at moments of crisis when the danger is clear and present. It happens even without a crisis when large numbers of people can see for themselves the evidence of a threatening trend. Dead fish floating in a dying lake, pockmarks on Grandpa's gravestone, and defoliation of a nearby forest compose a song without words about sulfuric acid in the atmosphere.

But on some issues, nothing that really affects you and me has happened yet. The looming threat arises from works of scholarship, illustrated by figments of the imagination. Epidemics show up first as statistics. Predictions of overpopulation stand uncertainly on the shifting sands of extrapolation. The case for worrying about the "greenhouse effect" rests on models of a global atmosphere so complex and fluid that even the fastest supercomputers are still no match for it. The Great Drought of 1988 was trumpeted as the first evidence of the greenhouse effect. But scientists are still trying to figure out whether it was evidence or an aberration.

For the global/behavioral issues not yet visible to the untutored eye, "we the people" cannot afford to relax until the scientists tell us what to think. Many scientists—though not, for the most part, those assembled for the Aspen symposium—want to be sure before they prescribe; but on global environmental issues that might be too late to prevent irreversible happenings. So we the people, once again by the millions, will also have to learn how to ask the "what if" questions—with the help of scholars and scientists whose stock-in-trade is peering into the future.

At the final session of the Aspen symposium, Noel Brown of the UN Environment Programme issued a challenge: "How about an Earth Situation Room—a data center wherein it is possible to collect the mass of information about the state of the planet and provide this information to all who care to find out?"

That night I had a dream: of a nongovernmental policy-analysis house in every town, connected by computer teleconference to the best available information—analyses, scenarios, alternative futures—on these global/behavioral issues. Anyone can

14

drop in and ask "what if" questions about global trends that might affect his or her own future, and learn what personal behaviors would make the unhappiest global outcomes less likely.

That kind of public education could help us all understand how true it is that everything we personally do has round-the-world impacts—and that every change in world health and the global environment has meaning for you and me and the precious species of which we are joint trustees. René Dubos had it right a couple of decades ago: Think globally, act locally.

■ ■ ■

Rapid and widespread awareness is not only imperative but possible, because of the big breakthrough of the 1980s—the marriage of computers and telecommunications in a variety of information technologies. The word can now get around in a hurry.

As a direct consequence of information technology, the international scientific community has discovered a common interest in "global change." "An ecumenical movement in the biological and earth sciences," Jack Eddy of the National Center for Atmospheric Research calls it, bringing together disciplines that have been focusing separately on the atmosphere, the oceans, agriculture, forestry, geology, geophysics, and outer space.

International science is now seeking to understand "Global Change" through what a National Academy of Sciences panel has called "a new effort to study the Earth and its living inhabitants as a tightly connected system of interconnected parts." This effort (its full name is The International Geosphere-Biosphere Programme: an Interdisciplinary Study of Global Change, sponsored by the International Council of Scientific Unions) "must be truly international, for the concerns of the program are those of the entire globe," according to the NAS report which touched off the ICSU initiative. "Considerations of access alone will require the participation of scientists and technicians from both the advanced and the developing countries representing all areas of the world. But a need equally great is that of the active involvement of the nations and the governments that must ultimately use the knowledge gained to make economic and policy decisions."

Is there a place in this excitement for those whose beat is the study of society and the management of organizations? There most certainly is. It's high time that the social sciences discovered a comparable common interest in "making a mesh of things."

The governance of the Global Commons—outer space, the atmosphere, the oceans, and Antarctica—is to social science what "global change" is to the natural sciences. In a word, it's the next frontier. Poised on this new frontier, it's hard not to be exhilarated by the tasks of institution-building that lie just ahead.

3

METAPHORS FOR THE COMMONS

A generation ago, people by the hundreds of millions were moved by the way the first space travelers described what they saw. They were not practicing poets but military practitioners, hard scientists, and engineers. But given enough perspective, the world we live in is evidently a lovely place. Seeing it from an unprecedented distance was an inspiring, for some an almost religious, experience.

"What a beautiful view." Those were the first words of Astronaut Alan Shepard, the first American to look down on us from outer space. Cosmonaut Gherman Titov was of the same mind: "Our earth is wonderful, the blue halo around it is very beautiful." Listen to Cosmonaut Andrian Nikolayev: "Our planet is uncommonly beautiful and looks wonderful from cosmic heights." And the immediate reaction of Astronaut James McDivitt from Gemini 4, when he first looked out and exclaimed: "Beautiful . . . beautiful! It looks great up here!"

The new fraternity of space explorers, since brought together by Rusty Schweickart in an international association, spoke not of nations, of continents, of islands, but of our earth, our planet, our world. They neglected to mention its divisions, but found it whole and blue and beautiful.

At the Aspen symposium Walter Orr Roberts spoke of this "totally new perspective," of our "new perception of the origin of comets, of planets, of some stars," and of the impact on our minds of looking from space, through the eyes and cameras and sensors of orbiting satellites, at the "fragile, fog-bound, beautiful Earth." Cyrano de Bergerac wrote of travel in a jet-propelled spaceship to the moon and the sun, and Jules Verne imagined a spaceship launched to the moon from Florida, near today's Cape Canaveral. A scientist who is also a philosopher, Walt Roberts also commented that "Perhaps it's too anthropocentric for us to call space a global commons. It might better be called a 'cosmic commons,' because it's not intellectually safe for us earthlings to assume that we're unique in the Universe."

The practical consequences of the first explorations of space have been enormous. The first Sputnik, a 184-pound payload launched on August 4, 1957, made hundreds of orbits of the earth, 90 minutes each at a speed of 18,000 miles an hour—followed by the first orbital passenger, the dog Laika, that flew in Sputnik II. Roberts reminds us of the "electrifying reaction around the world." Sputnik's demonstration of what was possible produced a gusher of government funds for science, engineering, and the teaching of exotic languages in the United States—and also, of course, huge public investments in the Soviet space program. It led to spectacular probes into deep space, the first men on the Moon, a variety of weather satellites, communications satellites, reconnaissance satellites, remote sensing satellites. It made possible many breakthroughs in scientific discovery such as the Van Allen belts, the magnetosphere, and clues to the composition of the sun. Since there is always a dark side as well as a bright side to scientific discovery and technological innovation, it led also to the use of space as the medium for the prospective delivery of weapons of mass destruction. And it has led to the new perspective that causes us now to consider "global environmental change"—on earth, in the oceans, in the atmosphere, in the sky beyond—as a whole.

■ ■ ■

This shift of perspective had nothing to do with the physical reality of our planet and its surround. The physical circumstances were all there before. The Van Allen belt was there (undiscovered and unnamed), the moon was shining, and the oblate spheroid where we happen to live was just as round and whole and blue before we looked at it that way. (Similarly, the laws of motion and the force of gravity were there before Copernicus and Newton and

Galileo changed forever the traditional notion that the Earth was the center of Creation.)

The difference now is that we have changed our minds, thus creating new metaphors with which to think. The wider perspective gained from the vicarious experience of looking "down" at the world-as-a-whole has induced a longer perspective as well. The systematic study of the future, still a very recent way of thinking, has brought into focus the long-term consequences of human activity, which is in turn made possible by our new willingness to think of the whole world at once.

As we now try to analyze and prescribe policy for the new *genre* of global/behavioral problems so characteristic of our time, it is well to have in mind that people's behavior is probably more influenced by myth and metaphor than by logic and reason. Even what starts as scientific reasoning can lead to misleading analogies—as in predicting for the Global Commons, in the post-industrial, information-rich environment of tomorrow, the kind of "tragedy" that overtook the common grazing areas in pastoral England in the preindustrial era.

■ ■ ■

The metaphorical mind of John Craven, ocean engineer and lawyer, takes our attitudes toward the ocean as a case in point. The ocean has been "a sacred cow," productive but off limits to our landlocked minds.

The ocean has certainly been productive for the human race, even without adequate management or understanding: "a low-cost bridge from world island to world island, a true commons for the harvest of marine protein, an environment for the assimilation of waste, the omnipotent God that regulates world climate, the thermodynamic machine that generates wind and rain and snow, and thus the rivers and streams that give us water and power."

For most people, says Craven, the metaphors for the ocean have to do with lurking perils, stormy weather, a place where vessels and people get lost, a place of death; oceanic art is symbolized by the wrath of Medusa. The Russian poet Lermontov captures the sense of dread:

The blue waves dance, they dance and tremble.
The sun's bright rays caress the seas.
And yet for storm it begs the rebel,
As if in storm lurk calm and peace.

But "with the new technologies of the ocean," Craven tells us, there does indeed "lurk calm and peace" in the stormiest ocean. "We discovered this when we first developed the true submersible, and found that once one is 150 feet below the sur-face of the ocean, one is in a benign, absolutely calm environment; one cares not whether there is a storm raging overhead, or a gale." And from this new perspective came the idea that a seagoing platform resting on submarine hulls could be as stable as most land surfaces (some of which, as in California, are not very stable at all). In one Hawaii experiment with stable platforms, the engineer's summary of his specifications was striking: It should be possible to play billiards in a 50-knot gale. (During the 1980s the Japanese have been developing that technology for a projected Marine Information City, but the U.S. government decided not to pursue it after the first successful experiments.)

Craven also objects to the put down of ocean potential that is inherent in our metaphorical preference for heights compared to depths. ("My thoughts rise up, my words stay here below. Words without thoughts, never to heaven go.") "Davy Jones's locker," the fate of the Titanic or the submarine Thresher or a German battleship, capture the public imagination. If we can build a road over Independence Pass, so people can look down at the world from the Continental Divide at 12,000 feet, says Craven, "we can afford to experiment with the technologies that permit people to see the ocean as it really should be seen."

We will find in the ocean commons, John Craven says, much nourishment (from mariculture and aquaculture), much energy (from ocean thermal differentials), much working space and living space (on stable platforms), and many new forms of recreation (in the underwater environment). But we are still stuck with the mindset of the poet Goethe, whose 200th birthday marked the origin of The Aspen Institute: "War, commerce, and piracy: these are the Trinity, one and inseparable, on the ocean."

We will only discover and develop the ocean's potentials, says Craven, if we abandon old metaphors that are out of touch with modern marine technology.

■ ■ ■

Awareness of threats to the global atmosphere has been, in the first instance, the product of scientific guesswork and observation; but these have been enormously multiplied by metaphors, which most people find more accessible than chemical formulas and computer models.

The first moves toward an international agreement to protect the ozone layer by controlling the emission of chlorofluorocarbons (CFCs) into the atmosphere were driven by scientific theories without much empirical basis. Parts of the chemical industry began to take the theories seriously, and some research was begun on substitutes for CFCs. But what caught the public imagination was the shocking discovery, by land-based measurements subsequently confirmed by satellite sensing, of a huge "hole in the ozone" over the continent of Antarctica.

For global warming, the initial metaphor was not well designed to promote behavioral change on a world scale. The idea of a "greenhouse effect" came from atmospheric scientists trying to explain in words of not more than two syllables the physical processes by which a part of the heat coming from the sun's radiation comes to be trapped and radiated back to earth by gases in the global atmosphere, placed there inadvertently by industrial civilization. The culprit gases—carbon dioxide, methane, chlorofluorocarbons and some other trace gases —act the way the glass roof of a greenhouse does; hence the popular analogy.

Not all scientists think the analogy is good science; Walt Roberts points out that there isn't any wind in a real greenhouse. But whatever its merits as science education for scientific illiterates (which is most of us), the "greenhouse" metaphor is plainly deficient as a people mover. For most people a greenhouse is a pleasant place where pretty flowers are grown under ideal conditions. The word fails to convey the pervasive perils of climate

21

change beyond all human experience within the lifetime of men and women already in their 20s.

At a 1988 conference on The Changing Atmosphere, convened by the Canadian government in Toronto, a better metaphor was floated by Prime Minister Gro Harlem Brundtland of Norway, the visionary politician who chaired the World Commission on Environment and Development. It's not a greenhouse, she said. It's a *heat trap*.

4

FAIRNESS IN THE COMMONS

At the same Toronto conference, the collision of logic with fairness was a primary focus of public speeches and corridor talk. Delegates from developing countries were blunt about it: the world's "North" emits the pollutants, the world's "South" is damaged. That overstates the case, because the "North" is damaged too and deforestation as practiced in the "South" is also part of the problem. But the question of compensatory offsets hung in the air: If we stop cutting timber and exporting it, a minister from Indonesia asked, who will help µs fill that big gap in our export earnings?

I heard no one in Toronto dispute that industrial countries produce three-quarters or more of the offending atmospheric gases, and that the poorer countries are disproportionately at risk. Consider: Just when the preindustrial economies are about to industrialize, the already industrial countries conclude that the cheapest fuels are too dangerous for the newcomers to use. Logical perhaps, but hardly fair.

Similar issues arose in the Law of the Sea negotiations; arguments about fairness versus free enterprise caused the last-minute breakdown of consensus on the Article about seabed mining. The Antarctic powers will have to deal with criticisms from outside their charmed circle. Negotiations about the allocation of radio frequencies, "parking space" at geosynchronous orbit, remote sensing from satellites, and the militarization of outer space have already produced debates rooted in arguments about fairness.

So the costs and benefits of actions to protect and develop the atmospheric commons will have to be shared in a manner widely agreed to be "fair." Otherwise the Global Commons will come to be an arena for bitter and continuous conflict.

■ ■ ■

"Are we organized to deal with the threats to the Global Commons?" The question was asked by Soedjatmoko of Indonesia, but the obvious answer ("No") is not just a challenge to public administration. It engages directly the issues of fairness or equity, among countries or within countries, that arise in the search for solutions to problems in a global family where some members are strong and some are weak.

Soedjatmoko dismisses out of hand the idea that fairness is essentially a problem between the world's "North" and its "South." The problem is that "the rich in the developing countries have more in common with the rich industrial countries than they have with the fate of millions of their countrymen who continue to live in poverty." A large part of the industrial world, and an important part of the developing world, "live in an enclosed universe of work and entertainment that has been made possible by the communications revolution, the growth of the media. They have very little to do with the problems of poverty that continue to afflict more than a billion people on this globe. . . . It's a gap between those who have access to modern knowledge and those who don't, between those who have work and those who don't. Those who don't have work and those who don't have access to modern knowledge are growing in numbers, rather than decreasing."

Eunice Durham, the Brazilian anthropologist, relates this fairness issue to the environment. What we have in common, she says, is "this common responsibility for destruction. . . . The poor and the rich, we are destroying [the environment] in different ways. The poor are destroying in order to survive, but this destruction leads to the persistence of the poverty which the destruction was supposed to alleviate." The rich "are destroying in order to preserve their wealth. But . . . this wealth will be unable to be preserved unless the resources are preserved and renewed."

The only way we can avoid the environmental destruction is to reverse the process that is leading to it, the process that makes the rich richer and poor poorer. "The destruction that leads the poor to recognize their poverty," says Eunice Durham, "is the same process that leads to the consumption by the rich which pollutes the environment from which the resources are taken. Only with a reversal in the patterns of consumption" by both rich and poor "will we be able to avoid destruction, and we cannot do that without having to deal with excessive wealth and excessive poverty."

■   ■   ■

The connection is thus quickly made between our common physical environment and our common humanity. But the threats and opportunities ahead, the product of the explosion of knowledge, have "not been accompanied by a commensurate explosion of human insight, restraint, and wisdom," as Soedjatmoko puts it. Just knowing more and more expands the areas of scientific uncertainty, and presses against "the social and cultural sustainability of our society."

"It will not be enough for us to conduct our business as if the problem before us is simply a matter of pushing back the borders of our ignorance through additional scientific research." We will need to enlarge our capacity to digest information, and develop "an enhanced power of conceptualization and integrative thinking," leading to "the kinds of decisions that leave open options. . . . One of the great lessons that humankind has to learn is that he does not stand outside the complexities of organic and inorganic systems in the world. He is part of those systems."

In his introductory comments at the Aspen seminar, philosopher Mortimer Adler had spoken with approval of the powerful universalizing trends. There is no doubt that the globalization of economic markets and the worldwide spread of ideas, enhanced in the 1980s by the marriage of computers and telecommunications, have deeply affected every society. But these trends are seen by many cultures, Soedjatmoko emphasizes, as "threats to their own integrity," and generate "an insistence on cultural or religious or ethnic identity." The result is "a crisis of intelligibility." It is the unavoidable tension (described by Lincoln Bloomfield and myself in *Rethinking International Cooperation*) between the technological push for wider institutions and the "inward pull of community"—not only geography-based states and ethnic nations, but dispersed communities of race, religion, economic interest, or professional solidarity.

Governance in a "crisis of intelligibility" has grown more and more difficult for single governments, however powerful. The traditional forms of governmental power—military deployments, economic planning, financial subventions, rules and regulations are increasingly irrelevant to the primary changes around us. World markets develop a life of their own. Environmental threats are increasingly global in their reach. Aspirations for freedom and pent-up frustration with official repression and ineptitude boil over, and political leaders have no choice but to accommodate popular sentiment; the drama in Eastern Europe that started in 1989 bears witness. Even before the Wall was breached, Soedjat-moko made the point: "Political philosophy, political theory, and political practice have been left behind by the realities of today and tomorrow."

The implications are radical, in the sense of getting to the root of the matter. The choices and chances in the Global Commons require extending our "moral horizons" not only to other peoples in our own time, but to the generations to come. "We either have a common future, or we have none."

In facing these choices and chances, we cannot depend on guidance from "the older religions, ethical systems, and philosophies," because our choices and chances did not exist when they were developed. "We will therefore have to learn," says Soedjat-moko, "to enhance our capacity for moral reasoning, to deal with problems" for which we cannot find "analogies in older, often petrified systems of wisdom." Unless we do that, we will be imprisoned in "obsolete, fossilized social and political structures"—and destined to work hard for our own demise. "What our humanness means for us is a world of very rapid change without fixed road signs." We will have to fashion our own road signs: "The future is an ethical category," because we choose it ourselves.

■ ■ ■

The familiar idea of a commons is a "public space," Professor Durham reminded the Aspen symposium. That implies equality of access, as in a village pasture or a national park. It also implies, indeed requires, public institutions to ensure equality of access while protecting the common resource from overuse—which was Garrett Hardin's "tragedy of the commons."

But that kind of commons, Durham points out, was "appropriated collectively." The four elements of the Global Commons are, so far, "unappropriated collectively." Thus the oceans, for example, have not been so much a place of cooperation as "a place of dispute, of war, of piracy. . . . It's controlled for the benefit of those who have the technology to use it." Maurice Strong reinforces the same point: "Are those who get there first with the technology going to preempt it for evermore? What do you leave for those who come second, who are simply not up there for the moment, but who are part of the greater commons of humanity?"

Freedom, this is sometimes miscalled. But "freedom of the seas" works out best for those with the power—the navies, the merchant marines, the fishing fleets—to use it. Similarly, freedom of trade works best for those with strong export-led economic strategies, and freedom of communication works to the advantage of those who do the most communicating (whether or not they happen to be those with the most to say). The common atmosphere is filling up with pollutants, mostly emanating from the technologically strong. Antarctic research is conducted mostly by the nations with strong science programs. The nations have agreed that none will appropriate outer space or celestial bodies, yet the limited space in geosynchronous orbit is becoming crowded with space vehicles that have distinctively national characteristics. And with the militarization of space, what Arthur C. Clarke calls "technoporn," there is likely to be peace in the heavens only as long as there is peace on earth.

Unlike the traditional commons (the pasture with too little grass to eat and too many sheep to graze), the Global Commons is inherently hard to "enclose." In consequence, the tragedy of the modern commons is less likely to lie in the depletion of its resources than in their collective mismanagement—the neglect of potential damage to fragile environments, and the inequitable sharing of benefits. In a study of Pacific marine resources, John Craven warns against ". . . the tendency to chop the [ocean] commons into manageable pieces, thereby risking its resources not being exploited for the benefit of humankind, but instead being wasted, intensifying preexisting inequities and providing a whole set of new occasions for international conflict."

The only places where something like a true commons concept now applies is where there aren't yet any people, or at least only a very few—where, as Eunice Durham says, "no settlement is possible . . . [or] where settlement is not very profitable." The ban on nuclear bombs in orbit was an early case in point. An arms control expert once said of the ban on nuclear weapons in Antarctica that it came to pass because the continent was occupied by penguins, not people. When minerals are discovered in exploitable quantities in Antarctica, will we have developed doctrines that assure some sharing of the benefits among those who have human needs, but lack the capacity to operate on that frigid and forbidding frontier? When human settlement comes to outer space ("the first extraterrestrials we meet will be our own sons and daughters," said an international lawyer at the earlier Paris seminar), will we have in place the institutions to avoid the division and appropriation of the "high frontier"?

"The moral problem is to create commons where they don't exist," Eunice Durham said at Aspen. She finds some hope in the technologies of communication and transportation, which "have created for the first time the concrete experience of a humankind . . . and a global world." She had just come from a public confrontation about the invasion of an Indian area with a project for a new airport; the sense of distant peoples colliding and cooperating is, she thinks, changing our perspective.

The idea of a commons is thus closely related to the danger that public spaces will be divided and destroyed—and to the chance to use such public spaces (if they can be protected from division and destruction) to achieve more fairness in a still unfair world. As the Brundtland Commission said in its report *Our Common Future*: "Inequality is the planet's main 'environmental' problem; it is also its main 'development' problem."

5

THE COMMONS AS A SYSTEM

How do we get hold of the idea of "governing" or "managing" anything on such a scale as the Global Commons? Comes Maurice Strong to the rescue with a solvent generalization: "The real commons," he says, "is not a place or a space but a system." It is the essential system of cause and effect on which human survival and well-being depend. It's like the human body. Every single component remains in place when breath leaves the human body, and yet "the stuff of life," which is the system, has stopped working.

In the *Encyclopedia of the Social Sciences*, "system" is defined as "a bundle of relations." The biggest bundle we can change (by changing human behavior, human policies, and human institutions) is the complex supersystem through which human activity interacts with the physical and biological and ecological systems. We cannot look at space, air, oceans, and an icy continent as separate commons areas, says Maurice Strong. "They are part of that larger commons, and you cannot deal with the commons except by dealing with the human activity which impinges upon them, and which takes place largely not within the commons, but in national sovereign states."

In this century, Maurice Strong points out, population has increased three-and-a-half times. But human activity, measured by energy use or industrial activity, has increased by 30 to 50 times— depending on which indices you use. That means that all the environmental damage so far, "the emerging symptoms of ill health in our planet and its life-support systems," are associated with levels of population and human activity much lower than they are bound to become. Four-fifths of the world's people "are just

29

at the beginnings of achieving their aspirations for further economic growth"—and people in the industrial world haven't given up their aspirations for better living either. "We must manage our future, or we are doomed. Human activity has reached a level at which it is now the decisive factor in shaping our future."

If the Global Commons is systemic, we need to identify what Maurice Strong calls the "boundary conditions" and "linkages" in the global system. Once the boundary conditions are widely understood, there is plenty of room for a pluralism of choices, a plethora of ideologies, as long as it is clear "what human activities impinge on those boundary conditions," and therefore who needs to do what, or stop doing what, to stay within those boundary conditions.

We don't know with any certainty the rate of change in the composition of the atmosphere, but we already know "within a reasonable range the limits beyond which we should not go. . . . That sets boundary conditions . . . for human viability, and we have to work back from that" to decide which human activities need to be changed, by individual decisions or social consensus or public control and discipline, in order to respect those boundaries.

Leaders in public and international affairs tend to speak in metaphors that will move large numbers of people. Maurice Strong is no exception. "We couldn't enjoy the freedom of the automobile if we didn't commonly agree on a set of boundary conditions: safety constraints, driving on one side of the road, stopping at red lights—a whole series of constraints which make possible the immense expansion of the range of choices which that technology provides."

He returns to the analogy of the human body as a system. What is a good regime for a diabetic—good exercise, a balanced diet— is good anyway for the diabetic's general health. "Now, when your doctor tells you your cholesterol is double what it should be, you've got high blood pressure, your heartbeat has got a murmur, you're overweight—he's not telling you you're going to die tomorrow, but you have to take him seriously.

"It's the same with our planet. We don't have an absolutely clear diagnosis, the evidence isn't all in. But the experts are telling us that our system isn't healthy, we are at risk; we have to take that seriously as a species." We have to act on the best judgment of the best "physicians" available. Ultimate judgment will never be available; that comes only with the postmortem—and "we simply can't afford to wait for the postmortem."

If Japan and Western Europe get along with half as much energy per capita as the United States does, it's clear enough that Americans can afford to do likewise; indeed, they can hardly afford not to, because we will keep losing the comparative advantage if we don't. Maurice Strong notes that in the 11-year period 1973 to 1984, Japan reduced the materials content of a unit of GDP by 40 per-cent, and did so while chalking up some of the highest rates of economic growth in the industrialized world.

He is impressed by the growing move toward "sustainable development" in Japan, and the enthusiasm there for pollution control technique. He quotes a Japanese businessman on environmental technologies: "This is the best thing for us to do economically."

"Whether it be energy use, water use, the recycling of waste, converting waste into raw materials, closed-system industrial processes—these are the wave of the future, they create exciting opportunities for scientists and for businessmen." Maurice Strong, a successful entrepreneur himself, recalls with chagrin that some business people opposed the abolition of slave labor and later of child labor, and opposed many health and sanitation rules—"but in the final analysis these were not bad for business or bad for the economy. . . . The business community is much more enlightened today, they're really in the forefront" of environmental sensitivity.

Doing what we should be doing anyway: that was a recurrent theme at the Aspen symposium—changing our habits of energy use and water use; preventing toxic chemicals from moving out into the food chain; conserving the cover of vegetation, not only in forests, not only in Brazil but closer to home. The threat of climate change gives us a whole new set of incentives to do what we ought to be doing anyway, like replanting forests and regreening deserts.

In this framework, adds Maurice Strong, "brotherhood, caring, sharing, working together are no longer simply pious ideals divorced from the realities of life, but the indispensable ingredients for human survival."

31

6

DIVERSITY IN THE COMMONS

The essence of our "common heritage" is the biological diversity of the planet Earth, what the Smithsonian Institution's Thomas Lovejoy calls "the basic library of the life sciences." He defines it quite simply as "the total number of animal and plant species." It's a term that can be used locally (the biological diversity of a puddle or a pond), or on the scale of a river system, a nation, or the globe. It cannot be treated as "a free and infinitely substitutable commodity"—like an acreage of pasture land—because "just by definition, one species is not substitutable in its entirety by another."

Tom Lovejoy's diversity map: Measured by the sheer numbers of species, most of our world's biological species arc on land and in its fresh water aquatic systems; mostly in the tropics; most of these, in turn, are in the tropical forests. These grow on 7 percent of the earth's dry land, and "may hold anywhere between 50 and 90 percent of all species of plants and animals." The range of numbers seems shockingly inexact; Lovejoy cheerfully concedes that "we have a tremendous problem with precision."

Whatever the absolute numbers, however, any substantial loss of diversity—that is, of "individual species which represent accumulated experience over evolutionary time," constituting "a series of solutions to unique sets of biological problems"—means throwing away "pretested biological systems" that embody important information about what works and what doesn't work. "So I would say the loss of great portions of biological diversity is an anti-intellectual act that makes the loss of the library in Alexandria trivial by comparison."

Except for migratory species, the diversity is clearly inside the borders of sovereign nation-states, where "a sense of possession dominates." The main issues here, Lovejoy thinks, are how to prevent useful information from being bottled up, how to ensure an economic return to the nations to whose resources the information can be traced, and how to prevent "the blockage of international collaborative research, which curtails the benefits to all societies from open study of biological diversity."

He cites an intriguing example: the knowledge that comes from the study of how the venom of the bushmaster viper works on its prey, to give them a case of "low blood pressure, zero forever." This reveals a whole system of regulation of blood pressure in the human species; using this knowledge, the Squibb company then designs a molecule which leads to a preferred prescription drug for hypertension, benefiting hundreds of thousands of people in many countries.

Another example of unforeseen benefits is an "insignificant little yeast" which takes toxic mercury out of streams in eastern Pennsylvania, reduces it to ordinary quicksilver and deposits it on rocks. Where there is lots of mercury pollution the yeast becomes abundant; when the stream is cleaned the yeast makes itself scarce again.

The moral of such stories is that "one can never say that a species in a community may not perform a useful function." Biological diversity is thus "our most sensitive environmental litmus paper." The definition of "sustainable use" has to be circular: if an area (say, a river valley) maintains its biological diversity over time, then there is sustainable use.

The trouble is, says Lovejoy, "looking at the globe from space" (there's that metaphor again!), human society has clearly exceeded the carrying capacity of the planet—as measured by biological diversity. The Brazilian Space Agency reports that 50 million acres have been burned in the Amazon alone, of which 20 million acres had been former tropical rain forests. Brazil's share of the problem is the largest "because Brazil has the largest chunk of tropical forest." If you add it up around the world, Lovejoy estimates that tropical forests are being destroyed at the rate of 100 acres per minute.

Fifty million burned acres might have released something like 600 million tons of carbon into the atmosphere ("an imprecise number, but a very large number"). This contribution to the greenhouse effect in turn "affects biological diversity by changing the physical conditions of the planet." And the rates of projected climate change, Lovejoy adds, "are faster than any which species have had any evolutionary experience with. . . . How we manage forests can help us, as we endeavor to muddle through to a solution to the greenhouse effect."

■ ■ ■

The focus just now is on Brazil—for good reason, says environmental planner Jose Pedro de Oliveira-Costa. Brazil and Colombia are the two countries with the greatest biological diversity, Brazil because it contains the largest amount of rain forest, and Colombia because it combines tropical environment with some very high altitudes that enhance the numbers of different species.

At Aspen he called attention to the difference between biodiversity and other environmental problems. Latin America is plagued with acid rain, oil spills, and all manner of problems resulting from the congestion of urban population—vehicle pollution, traffic jams, sewage, garbage, and the like. But these problems are reversible sooner or later. The loss of biological diversity is forever.

Oliveira-Costa is coordinator of efforts to save the remains of the much-decimated Atlantic Forest. He wryly observes that the Amazon is getting all the attention ("after we had been screaming for years, the *New York Times* has an editorial and suddenly everybody is interested"), but tells us that three special environments (including parts of the Amazon) merit the most urgent attention: the fragile eastern slope of the Andes, "much more at risk than Bangladesh"; the Swamp Zone shared by Brazil, Bolivia, and Paraguay, "flooded forests" for six months out of twelve, where a million crocodiles are killed each year "just for their skin"; and the Atlantic Forest, half in Brazil and the rest in Paraguay and Argentina, "one of the most endangered rain forests in the world," a microcosm of biodiversity containing 80% of the tree species to be found in Brazil, four of the most endangered primates, and all manner of mammals, birds, parrots, and plants.

There is potential here for "a kind of eco-tourism." There are 60 conservation units (analogous to state and national parks) that need to be improved. There is a need to create more "preserved areas." The good news is that Brazilian nongovernmental organizations concerned with the environment have multiplied from 20 or 30 ten years ago to more than 500 today. And Brazil's new Constitution, adopted in 1988, has a whole chapter on the environment; it declares the Atlantic forest, the Amazon forest, the Coastal Zone, and the central Swamp Zone to be the "patrimony" of all Brazilians, intended for use only in sustainable ways. But, says Oliveira-Costa, "international cooperation is fundamental."

Is there a role here for the "debt-for-Nature swap" idea, and if so how would it work? Most such ideas have in common that debt supposed to be paid in dollars is paid instead in local currency, the resulting fund protected against inflation, *to accomplish something in the debtor country that is internationally recognized to be valuable.*

The Brazilian government has already declared the Atlantic Forest to be something very special. Suppose a consortium of creditor nations should join with Brazil, and if possible other debtors (such as Argentina) to declare that forest a "global treasure." Part of what would otherwise have been debt repayments in foreign exchange would be converted into investments by the debtor nations *in their own currencies*, the resulting fund (supplemented by technical help and "ethical investments" from abroad) to be dedicated to preserving a forest even more endangered than the Amazon.

The fund's management would have to be international. But the "global treasure" idea, designed to mobilize help from around the world, involves no cession of sovereignty on the part of Brazil and its neighbors. The outside participants would simply be doing their part to help protect the Brazilian patrimony, in a joint effort to save a *national* resource of *global* value.

But first, of course, we would have to stop thinking of "the debt problem" as something to be bargained out between the two

36

parties most responsible for the mess: the debtor governments and the international bankers. The challenge is to broaden the conversation, widen the purposes to be served by a settlement, and open up a chance to convert debt into investment, repayments into development—and the "problem" into an opportunity.

■ ■ ■

Apart from the debt-swap idea, what other ideas are current and choice for the protection of biological diversity? Lovejoy points in directions that are both obvious and neglected:

■ Comprehensive surveys, to learn "where development can go without disturbing the planetary stock of plant and animal species."

■ Expansion of the number and coverage of "protected ecosystems."

■ More and better examples of sustainable development, alternatives for the landless poor so they don't have to destroy their nearby forests just to survive for a week or a year.

■ "Global management of forests," which leads to the global management of energy.

But these are "technical solutions," and they aren't enough. "We also have to think about the great social vectors of destruction"—population growth, social fairness inside countries, the gaps in trained manpower and in biological education. We should, says Lovejoy, "stop irritating Brazil over trade disputes when the big issue is how we can help Brazil move to collaborative world leadership in environmental matters." More sensitive forest policies in the United States would help too: U.S. policy in the Alaskan tundra reverberates around the world as a bad behavioral example. And we need to educate ourselves to think of economics and ecology as part of the same subject: "opportunity cost," a phrase much used by economists, should apply

37

to "all the opportunities that are foregone when biological diversity is destroyed."

This is serious business. You can't, says Lovejoy, "make a Xerox copy of the biosphere, and leave this one behind as a degraded toxic waste dump. . . . You can't negotiate with the environment."

7

ALARM AND UNCERTAINTY
IN THE COMMONS

There is already a striking consensus among scientists that if present trends continue our globe is going to get warmer— perhaps by an average of 6 degrees Celsius (much more at the poles, much less at the Equator) in a century or so. Such a change, so fast, would be without precedent in the history of climate as we know (and guess) it. We are not accustomed to thinking ahead a hundred years, yet that is within the lifetime of some children already born.

Almost everyone "knows" by now about the way carbon dioxide (CO_2) and other gases combine to produce a greenhouse effect that traps some of the sun's incoming radiation. So the more of these gases the atmosphere contains, the warmer the world of the future will likely be. The resulting "heat trap" could change the course of civilization in all sorts of unhappy ways—unless we learn how to slow the warming, or adapt to it, or (more realistically) both.

That prospect has produced in the 1980s an excited international dialogue; provoked a renewed interest in energy policies that don't depend so heavily on burning fossil fuels (the source of most of the emissions); generated worldwide concern about the destruction of the world's great forests (which store carbon dioxide when they are healthy and emit it when they are burned); and induced a close scrutiny of how emissions of other greenhouse gases (methane, ozone, fluorocarbons, etc.) can be limited by consensus or command.

Do we really "know" that what we are worried about is already happening? No scientific consensus here. That the six hottest years on record have all been in the 1980s is suggestive, but few experts are willing to go even as far as James Hansen, director of NASA's

Institute for Space Studies, did in his guarded attempt to sound unequivocal in testimony to Congress during that hot midsummer of 1988: "It is time to stop waffling so much and say that the evidence is pretty strong that the greenhouse effect is here."

At the Aspen symposium on The Global Commons, several of the leading scholars spoke of what we know and what we can't know until more time has passed or more research is done, or both. Ralph Cicerone, of the National Center for Atmospheric Research, spoke for the scientific consensus when he said the "forcing functions" (the physical and chemical reactions that are bound to change our future climate, and the effects they produce) are "real, they are sustained, they are growing, and they are directly related to human activities. . . . We know that the greenhouse effect works, and we know that it is accelerating. . . . Greenhouse gases are strongly correlated to human energy and human agriculture . . . correlated, probably proportionately or more, to human population and human quality of life." He added: "There is no magic thermostat to stabilize the earth."

■ ■ ■

A personal parenthesis: A few weeks after the Aspen symposium I visited the place where some of the key measurements of greenhouse gases are made. It's a lonely outpost of the National Oceanic and Atmospheric Administration (NOAA) on an almost empty stretch of lava at 11,000 feet on the upper slopes of Mauna Loa, Hawaii's biggest active volcano. The resource the laboratory studies is unique: air at its terrestrial purest.

Mauna Loa's clean air is captured by machinery atop a high steel tower and flows through a device that measures and records in a computer—each minute, around the clock around the calendar—how many parts per million (ppm) of CO_2 it contains. In other parts of the lab, other gadgets are figuring out, by examining batches of the mountain air, what traces of methane, ozone and chlorofluorocarbons are present.

All this started in the 1950s when a young scientist named David Keeling decided to measure CO_2 in the atmosphere, and wanted to do it where there would be a minimum of local pollutants in his samples of air. The Big Island of Hawaii was a good choice for a global standard of pure air: the trade winds travel for thousands of miles over open water just before they run into Mauna Loa. Even so, atmospheric purity is only relative. Nearby volcanoes keep spewing gases into the clean mountain air. The pollutants that human civilization always seems to produce occasionally break through the low clouds and reach the cleaner upper slopes. My host, NOAA's Elmer Robinson, pointed with a smile to a blip in his continuous graph: "That may have been your car when you arrived."

Keeling's 1958 machine is still there, laboriously tracing its findings with a mechanical pen on a roll of graph paper, supplemented now by much more sophisticated instruments, computerized display, and data storage. The work on the mountain is backed up by an analytical team in Boulder, Colorado, which compares the air in Hawaii with comparable measurements from the South Pole, American Samoa, and Point Barrow, Alaska—and from half a dozen other countries that now make similar observations.

I can report that on Thursday, August 31, 1989, there were 349.53 parts per million of CO_2 in Hawaii's mountain air. That compares with about 314 ppm in 1958, when Keeling's work began the series, and about 275 in the nineteenth century before the industrial countries started burning fossil fuels in a big way. The continuous upward trend is unmistakable and irrefutable.

The 1958–1989 Mauna Loa series, says Robert White, a former Administrator of NOAA, is "arguably the most important geophysical record of this century." It's sometimes called the "sawtooth curve," because in the Northern Hemisphere, the content of the atmosphere is higher in winter and lower in summer. (Summertime vegetation draws more of the CO_2 out of the air, and that factor is missing when many trees, bushes, and plants lose their leaves. Most of the world's deciduous trees are in the Northern Hemisphere.)

The curve, tracing the most important "greenhouse gas" for more than three decades, is now so widely accepted as proven fact that it forms the bedrock for a worldwide discussion of global warming and what to do about it:

41

■ The atmospheric sciences have mobilized to understand, and explain to the rest of us, the prospect of a warmer world.

■ Other scientists—biochemists, geophysicists, agronomists, bioengineers, oceanographers, computer modelers, and experts on fuels and forests and urban coastlines—have been galvanized into thinking about global warming scenarios.

■ Economic think tanks, government agencies, university departments, curriculum creators, strategic planners, educational foundations, agricultural associations, investment bankers, environmental lobbies, futurists, and the media have all had to put on their thinking caps anew, to consider how global warming may transform their traditions, assumptions, and political postures.

■ Corporations have to rethink their role in warming up the only earth we have—and also imagine what profit-making opportunities may present themselves in a warmer world. Residents of the Netherlands can hardly be looking forward to the sea level rise a warmer global atmosphere would bring in its train; but some Dutch engineers may be looking forward to the chance to advise other coastal communities on how to protect themselves with dikes, as the Dutch have long done so well.

The Mauna Loa Observatory costs the people of the United States about $400,000 a year. That's quite a lot less than what a healthy 25-year-old with a strong throwing arm might expect to derive from a season of effort in the marketplace for brawn with brains. The multiplier effect of the trustworthy numbers NOAA has produced and keeps on producing is incalculable, but enormous: It was those measurements that first clued us all into the probability of a warmer world. And the world's budget for all the coming efforts to retard and adapt to a warmer world will be counted not in thousands, but in billions or even trillions.

"Give me where to stand, and I will move the earth." So said Archimedes, explaining the power of a lever. A modern Archimedes needs no such mechanical fantasy for global leverage. Give me a few numbers everyone will believe, he or she might well say, and I will change the face of the earth.

42

■ ■ ■

At the Global Commons symposium, Ralph Cicerone showed the Mauna Loa curve, commenting that 80% of the emissions are due to the combustion of fossil fuels, the other 20% to all other losses of organic material, including those (like trees) that are burned. Other gases—methane, fluorocarbons—are present in quantities so much less than carbon dioxide that they are sometimes called "trace gases"; but their effect in building the global greenhouse is much greater (each molecule of methane, for example, is "worth" about 35 molecules of CO_2).

Projecting current trends to 2050 (always a precarious mode of analysis, since it requires an assumption that nothing will happen meanwhile to change the growth curve), the students of climate change find a world on which, in effect, the sun shines 1 percent to 3.5 percent brighter. (Again, an enormous range of uncertainty—remember Tom Lovejoy's *caveat:* "a tremendous problem with precision.") A smaller change [than 1 percent of the "solar constant"] "may have caused the Little Ice Ages in the opposite direction."

Stephen Schneider, also an NCAR scientist, reaches into ancient climatic history for perspective on the current numbers. In the last Ice Age it was only 5 to 9 degrees (Celsius) colder, on average, than it is today. But the "transition time" may have been as much as 10,000 years—which means a change of 1 to 2 degrees every thousand years, as a measure of "natural" change. But with the greenhouse effect we're looking at an increase of 2 to 8 degrees in a hundred years. That's 10 to 40 times the "natural" rate of change. "When we're that much faster, it would be sheer arrogance for us to say that we could predict the details, but it would also be sheer arrogance for us to assume that they're all going to be OK." If, for example, climate change speeds up, the forests (whose time scales are measured in hundreds of years) "are not going to be in equilibrium with the climate."

Schneider believes that "it's a better than even bet that we'll see unprecedented change into the next century." A one-in-two chance of catastrophic change does not lure even a betting man to wager on inaction. While not yet ready to say, from the physical

43

evidence, that the greenhouse effect is already being spread on the record by the weather we have all experienced in the 1980s, he does boldly, if in scientific prose, crawl out onto a limb for the '90s: "Sometime between 1990 and 2000 . . . the signal of the climate warming jumps out of the noise of the natural" climatic fluctuations.

■ ■ ■

So we can have a certain confidence (not "certainty," which is available only to evangelists and paranoids) that we are facing global climate change without precedent. But William Clark of Harvard brings us back to Earth: "There is no such thing as global climate change; nobody experiences it." For any individual or any society, the important changes are regional; and here the uncertainty level rises sharply. Moreover, there is an enormous difference in the capacity of human societies to adapt to rapid change: We can move agricultural crops quite fast, especially with the help of biotechnology and plant genetics. When it comes to energy systems, our capacity to adapt is much more sluggish. And the time scale for forest change is, as already noted, even slower.

Moreover, says Clark, other factors affecting growth and well-being and equity may well change even faster than the global climate. Population growth, for example, could "swamp" the impact of climate change; even in everybody's favorite extreme case, Bangladesh, half a century of global warming might flood 10 percent of its farm land, but the increase in the numbers of people trying to live off the land could be a much larger factor in creating crisis conditions. In the time scale of climate change (say, 50 to 100 years), there could also be a very great multiplication of technological efficiency and of economic activity, which again might be much more important than the slower impacts of climate change.

Having made the uncertainties clear, Clark nevertheless clarifies some likely regional trends. In the coastal zones, "the face of climate change will be erosion, and the intrusion of salt water." In the midlatitudes, the problems will be with forests rather than crops. In the higher latitudes, we can expect "real system transformation," deeply affecting not only agriculture but trans-

44

portation and resource development. "Marine transport prospects could open up considerably as the seasonality of sea ice backs off." And then there's military security, "the Joker in the deck." Hiding submarines under ice packs gains in importance "as technologies are able to detect submarines under water, even lots of water." (Consider also all the defense ramifications of melting ice in northern sea passages of special interest to the United States, Canada, and the Soviet Union.)

What should we be doing about all this, whoever "we" are? Policy options are the subject of the next chapter. But Clark leaves us with a useful way of thinking: "We would be exceedingly short-sighted, were we not to look at the kinds of activities that increase our robustness, our resilience, our adaptivity in the face of the climate and other environmental changes that are already in the cards."

8

POLICY FOR THE COMMONS

In the Global Commons "the scientific part is the easy part." So says Robert O. Anderson, the former chairman of ARCO and of The Aspen Institute. The rest of it, the policy part, is "the biggest challenge that ever faced civilization."

The scientists at the Aspen symposium did not argue the point; indeed, most of them were fluent with policy prescriptions for what "we" should do. Who "we" are exactly, and how "we" bell the cat, lacked precision, thus matching some of the forecasts in the science presentations.

Climate change is the integrating issue in the Global Commons, says Robert M. White, the first atmospheric scientist to become president of the National Academy of Engineering. If the Commons is the earth system itself, then "one can think of climate and climate change as the essential global environmental issue. Because in order to deal with climate, we must deal with everything that affects the climate, and that means dealing with almost the entire earth system—the oceans certainly, the biosphere, the tropical forests, and space. . . .

"As we look at the earth system and what humanity is doing to it, humanity's effect on the climate stems from the most basic functions of society: the production and use of energy, the production of food, the use of living and nonliving resources for economic development, the advancement of technology . . . the North-South debate on development, the management of the Global Commons, society's control of the direction in which technology should go . . . the deterioration and destruction of global ecosystems, issues of population control, transgenerational

47

effects. We will encounter all of these in the context of global climate change."

Policy for parts of the Commons was explicit or implied in much of what was said at Aspen. John Craven's essay on metaphors, discussed above in Chapter 3, is full of suggestions for what to do in the oceans. "Let's go to Mars *together*," Walt Roberts urged the international audience in his briefing on outer space; he also endorsed a Mission to Planet Earth for the study of global resources, pollution, the ozone layer, and the management of trash in space; he proposed Space Research Centers in Africa, Latin America, and Africa to help prepare people from every continent to participate in this shared new place for human activity; he stressed the need for widespread and continuous monitoring of "global change." Elsewhere in the symposium, there were references to the elimination of chlorofluorocarbons in industrial processes, and the need for deep cuts in the emissions that cause acid deposition.

But climate change, and especially the heat trap of global warming, did emerge at the Aspen symposium as the integrating issue to which all the stakeholders in the Global Commons, which are all of us, will have to address themselves.

■ ■ ■

Nobody thinks the warming of the globe can be stopped in its tracks. If the aim were to be maximum mitigation—to slow it as much as possible—what "boundary conditions" must be set? Steve Schneider suggests a "global emissions target." William Nitze, who was at the time of the Aspen symposium the U.S. State Department official responsible for thinking and negotiating about the global environment, put forward a quantitative concept for such a target: to make sure we stop well short of a doubling of preindustrial levels of "greenhouse gases" in the global atmosphere (expressing the very different kinds of gases in "units of carbon equivalent"). That means, he said, something like a 20 percent increase in their concentration compared to what it is now. This is the suggestion of Bert Bolin, the Swedish atmospheric scientist and science statesman who chairs the Intergovernmental Panel on Climate

Change, due to report on the whole subject in the fall of 1990. It tracks with similar recommendations dating back at least as far as an international workshop held at the University of Minnesota's Humphrey Institute of Public Affairs in 1981.

This tough standard would require sizeable cuts in emissions from the industrial countries to leave room for increases in emissions from peoples still in the process of industrialization, two billion of them in China and India alone. Such a standard of international fairness, says Nitze, might be regarded as an essential "political boundary condition."

In setting standards and organizing international cooperation to achieve them, the United States has to be the leader (the U.S. still does 85 percent of the world's climate research), and that will be possible only if we clean up our act at home. That will be far from easy, but it "will lead us to do a number of things that we should have done long ago for other reasons—and could usher in a technological, economic, and social revolution with potentially very positive consequences" for humankind as a whole.

The need for such a revolution, led by an American example, had been discussed for years by some members of the U.S. Congress; not many people were paying much attention. So the Senate Energy Committee, instigated by Senator Tim Wirth of Colorado with the indispensable support of Senator Bennett Johnson, the committee chairman, planned an educational hearing in the summer of 1988. Wirth picks up the story:

> What we did was call the National Weather Service and ask, "What, statistically, is the hottest day of the year in Washington?" The answer came back that it was in mid-June, so we scheduled a hearing on Global Warming for what was projected to be the hottest day of the year.
>
> The result was beyond our wildest dreams. The humidity was 100%, the smog factor was absolutely horrible, people could barely breathe. And we were, at the same time, in the midst of the heat wave in the Upper Midwest, the great drought that hit the country that summer. And instead of having the usual hearing in which you'd go into one of those Senate hearing rooms, and there

49

would be 8 or 10 people in the room, a couple of court reporters, the witnesses, two or three lost tourists, and that was all—instead of that, the place was jammed, standing room only, 14 television cameras, and Jim Hansen testified . . . . It was a seminal event in terms of public attention to the issue of global warming.

Very soon after that, [the newsmagazines] all ran cover stories on global warming. And I knew that we were making very significant progress when global warming made the cover of *Sports Illustrated.*

Despite the scientific uncertainties, the policy pioneers are proceeding on the assumption that the question about global warming is not whether, but how much and when. Senator Wirth and Rep. Claudine Schneider of Rhode Island have introduced bills for an Energy Policy Act (S. 234 and H.R.1078). Wirth's bill has been attacked by timber companies, utilities, automobile executives, and right-to-life groups. But members of Congress are hearing also from other constituents, and more than a third of the members of the United States Senate, from both sides of the political aisle, are now cosponsors of the bill.

Wirth's short list of essential actions is the product of much consultation with experts, so it matches the community consensus of expert opinion:

■ Better fuel efficiency. If Western Europe and Japan can achieve something like our living standard with half the energy use for unit of GNP, then we should be able to do as well. We might even be able to help others whose energy efficiency is worse than ours: The Soviets are half as energy-efficient as we are, the Chinese half as efficient as the Soviets, the Indians half as efficient as the Chinese.

■ Automobiles. They said it couldn't be done when the federal government set a standard of 27.5 miles per gallon, but that standard has now been met. Wirth thinks it could go to 35 mpg, and "then move up significantly beyond that." The energy savings involved are very large: ". . . for every mile per gallon increase in the efficiency of American automobiles, about 400,000 barrels of oil per day . . . the equivalent of two EXXON Valdezes every day." Bob Anderson demurs: it's technically possible to make a 50 mpg car, but he doubts that many Americans would want to drive it. Amory Lovins, on the other hand, says that at least nine automakers have tooled attractive prototypes in the 67–138 mpg range, with 200+ mpg on the drawing boards. They are, he says, generally peppier and cleaner that present cars; as safe or safer; and often quite comfortable. It's not just a question of size: he notes an Oak Ridge National Laboratory finding that of the doubling of new-car efficiency since 1973, only 9 percent of the saving came from reduced interior volume.

■ Fossil fuels. We ought to move away from coal and oil and toward natural gas. Incentives should be provided to that end.

■ Trees. If each child born into the world, says Wirth, were given 300 saplings, "and those saplings grew into full trees during that child's lifetime, they would absorb all the carbon dioxide that child would produce in his or her lifetime." There may not be room on the world's arable lands for that many trees, but the point is made vivid by a striking metaphor.

But here again, the United States has to clean up its act if it presumes to influence behavioral change elsewhere. We are tearing down, says Tim Wirth, "with your subsidy, 99 cents on the dollar," North America's last great rain forest, the Targass in southeast Alaska—"the greatest one-cent sale in history." (Two pulp plants process the timber, he adds; one is Japanese-owned, the other sends 95 percent of its product to Japan—courtesy of the American taxpayer.)

■ Alternative fuels. "Solar energy has reached all the targets we have set for it, and we've got to recommit ourselves" to its development. Nuclear power will have to play some role in the energy transition, but "the United States has got, for very good reasons, a kind of nuclear neuralgia. . . . We have an obligation

51

to think differently about this and so start all over again . . . to see if we can develop a nuclear technology that is safe, cost-effective, and addresses the issues of nonproliferation and waste."

■ Population. "Population growth is growing just as dramatically as the growth of CO_2 and . . . the destruction of the environment. . . . Direct correlation there, too." U.S. efforts to work with others on limiting population growth have slackened in the 1980s. We will need to turn that around.

■ International cooperation. Even if the U.S. were to become a perfect example, it accounts for only 25 percent of the buildup of carbon dioxide in the atmosphere. In the longer time-perspective, the most difficult part of the problem will be helping developing countries to develop without damaging the global environment as much as we have. That will require lots of "shared technology"; the kinds and degrees of transborder cooperation will "challenge . . . our diplomatic capability."

The proposals at Aspen from policy-conscious scientists form a similar agenda, with some additions. William Clark adds a need for "coastal structures"; for "moving cities back from the coast, as Charleston is slowly doing"; for thinking harder about agriculture, forestry, fisheries, and new urban habitation, especially in developing countries, and about the implications for transportation and military security already mentioned; and above all for developing "structures for fair compensation" that build more equity into "the extremely uneven and inequitable changes that climate alterations themselves will impose" on an already unfair world. Stephen Schneider comments that if "the market" will, as it must, be the main mechanism for changes in institutional policies and individual behavior, we have a lot of homework to do on the valuation of things we have never known how to value. "We don't know how to value wetlands, or how to value species."

In a talk at a Paris conference on Planet Earth a few weeks before the Aspen symposium, Frank Press, president of the

National Academy of Sciences, naturally advocated a "fast-track initiative to improve the science of climatic change, including studying historic natural changes, improving data acquisition, and enhancing understanding of the atmosphere-ocean system by conducting global experiments, improving modeling (with bigger and more computers), and attracting more scientists to the field."

But he went on to try the expert hand of a science generalist at building a short list of "initiatives that have merit independent of climatic change." Although it covers much of the policy ground covered also at Aspen, it is worth scanning because Frank Press tried also to put a price tag on his package:

A major push to reduce CO_2 emissions by energy efficiency;

Improved water efficiency in agriculture and industry;

R&D initiatives in support of nonpolluting, safe alternate energy sources, tilting toward them when feasible;

Biotech initiatives to genetically engineer food plants to use less water and fewer chemicals;

A survey of the nation's water resources and water use policies, and preparation of preliminary plans for hydrological initiatives;

Coastal zone management incorporating an anticipation of sea-level rise;

Reforestation driven by the dual needs to preserve species diversity and to reduce atmospheric CO_2; and

Chlorofluorocarbon cutoff and replacement by safe alternatives.

"The cost of all these measures," says Press, "is a few billion dollars a year, manageable, and justifiable as prudent," considering that "humankind has become a more important agent of environmental change than nature."

■ ■ ■

Cost—ay, there's the rub. The gathering consensus on what to do is stretched to the breaking point when it comes to paying for it.

Darius W. Gaskins is an academic and government economist who became President and CEO of Burlington Northern Railroad. He acknowledges the perspective of his responsibility: "We make more than 50 percent of our profits by hauling low sulphur coal to utilities for generating electricity." If it turns out that the United States has to eliminate burning coal to produce power, "it will have a devastating effect" on Burlington Northern.

Gaskins agrees that global warming is real, despite all the uncertainties. But he thinks that the policies being discussed would be "costly and disruptive." There can be costs in delaying action too, for example in the loss of biological diversity. But he argues that it's hard to move people if you don't have a general consensus, and that it's especially hard to do "draconian" things in a decentralized economy and a popular democracy. (Congresswoman Claudine Schneider later urges the danger of "prejudicing consensus with words like 'draconian,' which elicit the reactionary mode of scare tactics.")

From long experience as a government regulator, Gaskins wisely urges caution about freezing public policies into administrative rules. "They always seem to end up having unforeseen consequences . . . it's real hard to change any kind of economic regulation in an industrial society like America, once you put it in place. . . . Everybody reacts to the regulation, makes investments in one technology or another, in one house or another, in one beach front property or another." Economic regulations, he says, tend to have a half-life of 25 to 50 years, so any new regulatory regime should be written to retain as much flexibility as possible.

The policy conclusion? Reduce "the band of uncertainty"; get a much better understanding of the costs to be incurred, and by whom; focus hard on *adaptive* strategies, because whatever happens we won't be able to mitigate as much as we would like; "maintain trust among ourselves" in order to reach for consensus; and strengthen the Global Commons concept.

Economist Gaskins is encouraged that "man is not merely an economic being," that self-interest is not the only available motivator for behavioral change. He also finds in the explosion of information an "optimistic note": "As information filters through the world, we have a much better chance of affecting the body politic in all the nations that have to make the big changes."

Amory Lovins, longtime advocate of energy conservation, is at the other end of the spectrum of opinion on what to do and how to do it. The scientific uncertainties are "legitimate, but largely irrelevant . . . we should do, essentially, all the same things regardless." The important thing is not to "fiddle while coal burns."

"Abating global warming, far from being costly, will probably, on the whole, be highly profitable," says Lovins. "Full use of the best demonstrated (but not yet all on the market) oil-saving technologies can save about four-fifths of U.S. oil use at an average cost below $3 per barrel. Full use of the best electricity-saving technologies on the market can save three-fourths of U.S. electricity, more cheaply than just *operating* a coal or nuclear plant, even if building it were free. Most of the best electricity-saving devices now on the market were not available even a year ago. The cost-effective potential of saving electricity has improved roughly sixfold in the past five years, and almost thirtyfold in the past 10 years." So the cost of abating global warming, since it is profitable, should largely "be done through the market, not through mandatory regulation."

"The Swedish State Power Board just published, shorn of the usual disclaimer, a description of how moderately efficient use of electricity, fuel-switching, and environmental measures could simultaneously expand GNP by 54 percent, phase out nuclear power (which is two-fifths of Sweden's power supply), reduce carbon dioxide output by a third, and cut the cost of electrical services by nearly $1 billion per year—all at the same time. . . .

"Since the average poor country is only about a third as energy-efficient as the average rich country, and we now know how to make the rich countries at least four times as efficient as they are now (very profitably at present energy prices), developing countries that do it right the first time—which will need a lot of help from both sides—ought to be able to grow their economies roughly tenfold without increasing their energy use at all, while we decrease ours severalfold with no cut in our standard of living."

The technological optimism of Amory Lovins always leaves his audiences breathless, and so it was at the Aspen symposium. But over the years he has mutated from the *enfant terrible* of energy policy to a prophet with many followers, including dozens of utility clients. Even skeptics who have learned from bitter experience that lunch is never free find it increasingly hard to dismiss the vision of an energy future that promises to solve the puzzle of global warming in ways that make it a positive-sum game.

■ ■ ■

The costs of policy change in the Global Commons obviously have to be faced as squarely as the benefits. But just as obviously, the costs of behavior modification that would come anywhere near matching the scale of the problems described at Aspen are by far the most sensitive issue in every expert mind. In reviewing my notes on the Aspen symposium, I am struck with a small but possibly significant irony: the only explicit reference to "a carbon fee or energy tax of some kind" came from an official in the executive branch of the U.S. government.

But the bottom line is still what people—millions of people— will be willing to do, or stop doing. So the essence of global/ behavioral change is the pervasive spread of knowledge, because people-in-general have to get the idea before the policy announcers (intellectuals, politicians, government officials, corporation executives, community leaders) can summon the courage to "make policy." In this perspective, what happened in Eastern Europe in 1989 is a metaphor for what could happen in the 1990s in the Global Commons.

9

CONSENSUS AND COHESION
ON THE COMMONS

Let us not follow where the path may lead.
Let us go instead where there is no path,
and leave a trail.

Japanese proverb

Will the degree of consensus sustain a coherent framework for global action? Large scientific uncertainties remain. The scientists, already a global community in fact and in feeling, will continue to chip away at them—and each new insight will doubtless uncover wider areas of ignorance requiring new discoveries, in the endless and exciting pursuit of elusive truth. Meanwhile, what do the world's citizens (including scientists acting as citizens) do about what we already know and guess and believe?

When in Samoa the villagers all gather to make some important decision, they argue and listen and argue and listen some more. But there comes a moment when the participants look to a respected village elder to formulate their consensus. In our microcosmic global village, Walter Orr Roberts was a "natural" to speak for the group. At the Aspen symposium he suggested nine points of convergence:

1. In the matter of the Global Commons, "we are beyond the point of needing more research before acting. . . . There are, of course, great benefits in more research to reduce uncertainties and to define strategies to cope and to benefit. But we need to act on what we know now."

2. There are many strategies to "moderate the global 'hot box,' and they will ensure the planet's hygiene no matter what

57

happens." That is also true for strategies of adaptation, which Roberts thinks should get at least equal billing with prevention. (There was a striking absence, at this Aspen meeting, of the customary debate about prevention *or* adaptation, as mutually exclusive kinds of policy and action. Nearly everyone who spoke about global warming seemed to want some of both. That in itself is an important advance in consensus.)

3. The concept of a Global Commons is endorsed as a new and more inclusive framework for thinking. "It is time to renew, revitalize, and refine the concept of the commons, not only the physical/biological commons of air and sea and space and Antarctica, but also the idea of an Information Commons." [See Part II, below.]

4. "It's extremely important in this day and age . . . to give additional attention to complex adaptive systems working as integrated wholes. All too much in the past, we've looked at the components and considered that the whole is the sum of the components. The whole is much more than that."

5. We should "emphasize fairness in all our thinking about strategies for control and for adaptation."

6. "There is still great importance to monitoring how we're doing globally," using "new information technologies to make data available in concise, usable, and digestible form."

7. "Nongovernmental approaches" and "pluralistic mechanisms" will be of the essence in managing global change.

8. As a sequel to the United Nations Conference on the Human Environment, held at Stockholm in 1972, there will be another world conclave on the Human Environment in 1992. "Perhaps some sequel to this Aspen meeting can play a role" in the careful and imaginative preparations that will have to be made for the 1992 Conference. (Maurice Strong served as Secretary General of the 1972 Conference. He had earlier celebrated The Aspen Institute's creative role in organizing a

drafting session, convened by Walter Orr Roberts and Thomas W. Wilson, Jr., which greatly helped to frame the 1972 Stockholm Declaration.)

9. "A very high priority is to plan educational measures on the concept of the commons," activities aimed at "patterns of behavior and the value systems of the peoples of the world, with emphasis all the way from kindergarten to adult education." The media, political leadership, and nongovernmental organizations all have a role to play in pushing education for the Global Commons."

■ ■ ■

We have assumed that the human race is somehow responsible for—people used to say "master of"—the earth, the seas around, and the skies above. In each part of the interconnected Global Commons, issues of governance arise. They cluster around three questions:

Who will explore?
For what uses?
For whose benefit?

Variants of these questions preoccupied UNCLOS III (the most recent Law of the Sea negotiations, 1967–82). They will bedevil the 1991 review of the Antarctic Treaty. They will move center stage in the management of weather resources as we learn how to modify the weather at human command—and continue to change the climate by inadvertence. And they are central to any consideration of the governance of outer space. At the outset of the Space Age, we said "We will take no frontiers into space." Yet the exploration of space so far has been a nation-based "space race."

A global interest can be defined. It has been defined as a matter of international law in the oceans and outer space—but, curiously, not in the atmosphere. Now there are moves to create a Law of the Atmosphere. Three basic assaults—acid rain, ozone depletion, and global warming—are driving nations toward cooperation.

59

Should we impose our values on still-vacant environments? We pondered this philosophy at the earlier Paris workshop. The answer that emerged was: How could we do otherwise? "What we love results in what we do," said one participant. If in the oceans and the skies we don't "impose values such as environmental prudence, protection of diversity, and a balance of human rights and responsibilities, then we would replicate in the Commons the earthly conflicts that would make the Commons merely a new theatre of war." In the Commons above all, added Jens Evensen of Norway, a justice of the World Court, "mankind has a right to peace."

The governance issues remain. By "governance of the Commons," do we imply:

■ that the Commons is like a garden, where everything is "managed"? I have heard the Global Commons described as "a string of global parks." But do we know enough to organize a Global Park Service? Can we develop the doctrine required to train ourselves as global park rangers? The admonition of wise man Lao Tsu, 2,500 years ago, is still wise: "Do you think you can take over the universe and improve it?"

■ that we had better arrange not to touch it because we may upset what millions of years of evolution have created? This is the "wilderness" approach, driven by a paralyzing sense of our own ignorance and a healthy respect for the "foul-up factor" in human affairs.

■ that as a practical matter the Commons won't be left alone, but as an equally practical matter a world consensus is required in these nobody-in-charge environments? This option is probably the only one realistically available to us. But it requires, if not "management," at least balancing our appetite for adventure and our ambition to expand human civilization's physical frontiers with a sober awareness of what one of our Paris participants called "our ignorance, our dependence on the wilderness, and our shared need to protect the 'uncommons.'"

In all this, what is the role of public governance? "The private sector can do most of the job," says Maurice Strong—just as it already does (in some countries such as the United States) in designing and building weapons and providing for many health and social services. But government is needed "as rule-maker, as manipulator of incentives and penalties," setting boundary conditions and arranging linkages that are essential for societal survival and health and prosperity, but encouraging nongovernments to do the rest.

"Is the market principle compatible with a secure Earth?" The question is posed, without implying a judgment, by Noel Brown, the Jamaican who has long been New York representative of the U.N. Environment Programme (UNEP).

These two comments, taken together, suggest a two-tier principle of international cooperation. In the "Rethinking International Governance" project, we have described such a system generically as follows:

(a) a more centralized process with universal participation, where debate is encouraged and agreement is reached on standards, norms, goals, and codes of ethics; and

(b) the more operational level, where many different enterprises and authorities can "do their own thing" within the framework of the agreed standards/norms, without the need for international decision making or bureaucracy.

The link between the two tiers is international systems for monitoring adherence to the standards/norms—the data being widely distributed. In 1978 President Giscard d'Estaing of France proposed to the United Nations an International Satellite Monitoring Agency which could verify arms control agreements (that is, doing what the United States and the Soviet Union were already doing for themselves) and help defuse peace-and-security crises. It's still a good idea. Independent international observation of agreed environmental standards/norms could operate on the same principle; indeed, with information provided by so-called national technical means, UNEP is already doing some environmental monitoring.

The important thing is that such observations be freely available to whoever wants them. In a speech endorsing the

French proposal, scientist/novelist Arthur C. Clarke said it would help the world enter an "Age of Transparency. Like most people, many nations would not like to live in glass houses." Considering the capability of reconnaissance satellites, or even of the French SPOT satellite, which could detect from space the white line down the center of a runway at London's airport, they may not realize, Clarke says, the extent to which they are already living in glass houses. "As the Age of Transparency dawns, political and military wisdom will lie in cooperating with the inevitable."

The commons environments, and the dangers of degradation and conflict that arise from them, quite evidently require the establishment of universal norms and standards. But their actual conservation and use will of course be in the hands of hundreds of governmental units, thousands of public, private, and "mixed" enterprises (national and local regulatory agencies, corporations, science academies, advocacy organizations, laboratories, universities, etc., etc.), and ultimately in the hands of millions of schoolteachers, hundreds of millions of householders and automobile owners, and billions of people raising their living standards . . . and their expectations.

But if all of these are going to improvise in their pluralistic ways on a general sense of direction, and if that improvisation is going to be fair to the technologically weaker peoples of the world community, widely agreed "rules of the road" will have to become international public policy. And the key improvisers, who can make or break the system according to how they act, will have to be brought into consultation about the norms and standards if they are expected to abide by them.

■ ■ ■

Those who cry havoc about the global environment are sometimes startled by the dramatic effect on their forecasts of people heeding them. It took only 13 years to get from the first scientific guess (in 1974) that chemicals released by certain industrial processes could damage the layer of ozone that protects the human race against skin cancer and other ultraviolet harm, to a treaty signed in Montreal in 1987 which begins the phase-out of chlorofluorocarbons in the chemical industry worldwide.

Is the Montreal protocol a model for the setting of norms and standards on other problems of worldwide concern in the Global Commons—for example, getting a solid agreement on setting an "outer bound" for the global emission of greenhouse gases, and on how the resulting costs and burdens will be shared?

Some of those gathered in the Aspen symposium think it was "too easy" a case. What needed to be done could be accomplished if the governments of major industrial nations and a few other key players (such as executives at Dupont and some other chemical companies, who were belated but necessary converts to the idea of phasing CFCs down and eventually out) could agree. Darius Gaskins thinks a more likely model is the laborious process of trade negotiation—"and that's scary," he adds, because the mechanism is creaky, to say the least. But he concedes that another model, that of arms negotiations, is even creakier.

Richard Benedick, a major player himself as head of the U.S. delegation to Montreal, argues that it all looks easy only in retrospect. An important precedent was set by the ozone agreement. "It was the first time the international community was able to agree on controls on a very important set of chemicals, before there was any measurable evidence of harmful effects. This was not a response to an ecological disaster such as Chernobyl, but rather a preventive action on a global scale."

He cites four lessons to be learned. First is "the importance of building an international scientific consensus. And this involves . . . a close linkage of scientists with policy makers and with diplomacy. This is a very uncomfortable role for modern science, but it's one they have to accept."

Second, it is necessary for information to flow fully both to leaders and to the general public—whose actions or restraint ultimately determine how far leaders can agree with other leaders.

Third, "there was an innovative fact-finding process—a series of informal international workshops," running right up through the formal negotiations themselves. Those engaged in the search for norms and standards were "people from all parts of society: government, industry, academia, science." In these workshops the problem was "disaggregated," which was better than "trying to solve everything at once." In this process, UNEP served as a center of initiative, playing "an essential catalytic, mediating role"—as it did in the 1970s in mediating the cleanup of the Mediterranean Sea. The same, says Benedick, will have to be true on the issue of climate change: the United Nations will have to be somewhere near the center of the picture.

Finally, Benedick cites the innovations in the treaty itself. It does not legislate specific solutions, but allows room for the market to develop economic incentives that should push CFC emissions in the right direction: down. The treaty tries to deal with fairness by establishing a slower transition period for developing countries. And, "most important and innovative of all," the treaty provides for "reopening the timetable and changing the schedule of CFC reductions . . . a deliberate design of a flexible and dynamic process."

The Montreal treaty process illustrates, admittedly in microcosm, a role for nongovernments that will be increasingly important in the future history of international cooperation. In a world politics with nobody in charge, the role of nongovernments and of enterprising public citizens expands from day to day. The global flow of digitized information is under no government's control. Governments do well to keep up with what the nongovernments are doing, let alone track their billions of daily transactions.

Global companies move resources around to take advantage of changing skills, supplies, transport—and fluctuations in money values. Environmentalists come together to pressure the World Bank. Geophysicists measure in common the world we share. Atmospheric scientists model the climate and consult about ozone and carbon dioxide. Microbiologists consider a code of ethics for biotechnology. Publishers gather to sell books and complain about unenforceable copyrights. Police agencies assemble to internationalize the tracking of criminals. Drug traffickers consult across frontiers about new ways of evading their national police. And fanatics coordinate their next targets for terror.

One solid prediction can be made about conflict and cooperation in the Global Commons. Governments are losing their grip; nongovernments are coming on strong.

■ ■ ■

Toward the end of the Aspen meeting, Soedjatmoko returned to the fairness theme. Whether or not information should be considered as another kind of commons (see Part II, below), it's clear that an enormous "knowledge gap" exists. "People in the Third World, governments as well as nongovernments and the public at large, are very much preoccupied with their own problems, their own development efforts, and have shown so far very little interest in the changes that affect the global life-support systems for humankind. There is therefore no strong political constituency that would make it possible for governments to act effectively and with enthusiasm. . . ."

So "building scientific and technological capabilities" in the developing world is a first essential, along with development theories that link Third World development to the health and hygiene of the Global Commons. The problem in most developing countries is cohesion; but social science has emphasized social analysis, by "decomposing" societies. It's important that institutions such as the Third World Commission and the Third World Academy of Sciences undertake studies on their own about the Global Commons, and participate in worldwide discussions on the subject.

Soedjatmoko chides us, gently but firmly, with focusing too much on the United States, simply because the U.S. data are better and the policy issues are already cover-story news. It's true, as several U.S. speakers had said, that the United States should set an example in order to be able to provide credible leadership on issues in the Global Commons. But "problems of this scale do not lend themselves to doing first this and subsequently something else. . . . We will have to solve our problems together."

Missing in the discussion, he thinks, is "the likelihood of massive population redistribution across the globe." That's a world in which hundreds of millions of people from crowded countries (China, India, Indonesia, Nigeria, Egypt, Mexico, and Haiti, to name the most obvious) might come to think of moving to the comparatively empty countries (Soviet Asia, Australia, Canada, the United States) as a human right born of overpowering human need. Among its many other impacts, global warming alone would both force and facilitate that kind of global change.

But Soedjatmoko focuses his special eloquence on the need for democratic decision making. Will it be possible, he asks, "to resist the inclination, given the long time-frame within which people have to learn to adapt and adjust, to use coercive methods to change human behavior?"

"One of the problems is that the scale on which we will have to develop systems of cooperation makes it impossible for us to be very choosy about who our partners in this cooperative process are going to be. We can't afford to exclude regimes we don't like, because there is this overriding common interest of human survival. This will be one of the great moral challenges in our efforts to deal with these problems of human survival." Can we, Soedjatmoko asks, avoid autocratic solutions in reacting to catastrophe? It's not enough to survive; we have to "survive with freedom."

We can take heart, I wrote in a note to myself, from the fact that the Chernobyl disaster was an important impulse to Mikhail Gorbachev's conversion to environmentalist, and to making *glasnost* a part of Soviet foreign policy. "They say that one thorn of experience is worth more than a whole forest of instructions. For us, Chernobyl became such a thorn." Thus wrote Gorbachev in his extraordinary article for *Pravda* and *Izvestia* on September 17, 1987. None of us is secure, he wrote, "when currents of poison flow along river channels, when poisonous rains pour down from the sky, when the atmosphere polluted with industrial and transport waste chokes cities and whole regions, when the development of atomic engineering is justified by unacceptable risks." For a moment there, I thought I had picked up the Sierra Club newsletter by mistake.

■ ■ ■

"The world is inching its way toward a new consensus," says Noel Brown. "The environment is fast moving to the top of the world's political agenda. An increasingly impatient global public is demanding that governments and society do more now to protect the global environment and its life-support systems."

A new kind of leadership will arise, he thinks, which is willing to treat fairness, or equity, as a political claim. "It's easy to talk about poverty, but poverty is a condition; equity is a claim." Those who have enjoyed the largest benefits and wreaked the most planetary destruction surely have a special obligation as well. The political claim is not only for equity in our time, but for "intergenerational equity." "Will the children of the future be consigned to a kind of Third World status?"

Beyond human rights, there is the equivalent concept of human solidarity, a "fairly new concept that transcends national boundaries and national sovereignty, and may yet be the cement" that binds us together. . . . "If the Global Commons is truly the living Earth, then its protection becomes a global human responsibility that we should try collectively to discharge."

Noel Brown is into metaphors too. "We seem to lack a global unifying myth. Global warming may yet become a unifying theme." He looks for help to the primary salesmen of metaphors. "In shaping the new agenda for the earth, we should look to a new constituency, arts and the entertainment media." If the new planetary issues are both global and behavioral, the communications that reach the widest audiences have the greatest potential for developing cohesion and consensus on the Global Commons.

PART TWO

■ ■ ■

Information
as a Commons?

10

THE BRAINWORK COMMONS

We have seen that the fusion of computers and electronic telecommunications made possible a new perspective, new exploration, and new exploitation of the physical and biological commons. We have seen a new idea catching on, that four huge parts of our natural environment—outer space, the global atmosphere, the deep ocean and its seabed, and the continent of Antarctica—should be treated as a Global Commons, belonging to nobody or everybody and therefore a shared responsibility: the "common heritage" of humankind.

But if the mark of a global commons is that it cannot readily be divided or appropriated and that it requires an unusual degree of international cooperation to be explored or used at all, there is another candidate for treatment as a global commons: the worldwide flow of information and especially digitized data.

Pierre Teilhard de Chardin spoke of the envelope of knowledge around us as the "noösphere"; he added it to the natural "biosphere" and the "technosphere" of human artifacts, to make a complete picture. Kenneth Boulding defined the "noösphere" as "the totality of the cognitive content [and] values, of all human nervous systems, plus the prosthetic devices by which this system is extended and integrated in the form of libraries, computers, telephones, post offices, and so on."

The accumulated lore of civilized humanity, not only "recorded history" but the know-what of scientific inquiry, the know-how of technology, the know-why of values, and the know-who of social institutions—not to mention our hunches from unremembered subconscious learnings—is certainly part of our common heritage." New information technologies have quite suddenly

71

multiplied our capacity to store knowledge about the past, to communicate present knowledge, and even to simulate future knowledge.

So while we are puzzling about the governance of the shared environments in the waters, and the sky around and above us, we had better reserve some of our imagination for that other ubiquitous, fluid, shared environment, the global flow of information.

■ ■ ■

The backdrop for considering an "information commons," like the scenery in Aspen, is dramatic. Suddenly the ice floes of frozen ideologies, imprisoned human minds, and neglected human needs seem to be breaking up.

Two hundred years after the French Revolution and the beginning of constitutional government in the Western Hemisphere, political choice is busting out all over. Educated people by the millions—to use the Chinese categories: students, workers, intellectuals, professionals—seem determined to have a voice in their own destiny. The ambitions of newcomers will always be resisted, in the short run, by those who already have it made. In the longer run, they will prove irresistible—in the shipyards of Gdańsk and the Soviet Academy of Sciences yesterday, in Eastern Europe today, and tomorrow in Burma, South Africa, Central America, and China.

What has produced this demand for democracy is mainly the spread of knowledge, the revolutionary impact of getting millions of people, especially young people, educated to think for themselves, enhanced by the increasingly widespread use of modern information technologies. Do we need a better example than the modern Chinese opera that we all witnessed in the summer of 1989? It was no accident that those huge and impressively self-disciplined crowds were led by the "the students." In the global information society, education is the kinetic energy of the future.

Informal networks, using radio and facsimile and motorcycle couriers, bullhorns and word-of-mouth, passed information around Beijing at astonishing speed, and spread it rapidly to Shanghai, Xi'an, and other population centers. Television, radio and telephones and facsimile also got the word around the world in real time—not just the organized media networks, but to an extraordinary extent, networks that spread information widely and directly to friends and relatives abroad.

The Chinese uprising may, indeed, go down in technological history as the world's first FAX revolution. And when the Chinese government decided that it simply had to choke off those damaging television images, it was still largely powerless to strangle photocopying, shortwave radio, telephone calls, and FAX transmissions without also strangling China's newly interdependent economy.

During a newscast from Beijing, in May 1989, I opened my dog-eared edition of the *Tao Te Ching* at random and found this relevant little paradox, written by Lao Tsu 2,500 years ago:

When the country is ruled with a light hand,
the people are simple.
When the country is ruled with severity,
the people are cunning.

Elsewhere Lao Tsu used an even homelier metaphor: "Ruling a big country is like cooking a small fish"—that is, too much handling will spoil it.

■ ■ ■

Of all the happenings of this extraordinary time, I think the most important, by far, has been the marriage of computers with telecommunications—the great event for which the 1980s are most likely to be remembered. The happy couple had been making waves together since the 1950s. But it wasn't until the '80s that what Albert Bressand, a French economist, calls "a technological shockwave, with information processing as its epicenter" really lashed the shorelines of the nation-state.

Data networks of extraordinary speed and complexity already link commodity traders, airline ticket agents, air traffic controllers, weather forecasters, public health officials, currency speculators, modern librarians and multinational executives with each other.

The participants in these networks, whether in public or private employ (if you can any longer tell the difference), are tolerant of governments but operationally independent of them. The international exchange of money is already a worldwide, 24-hour-a-day market, in which it doesn't matter where you are, as long as you or your associates are awake and plugged into the global flow of constant communication. The grain merchants already have an intelligence system that, on subjects on which they have a special interest like the internal politics of Argentina, probably overmatches the combined capacity of the CIA and the KGB.

An economist in Zurich now guesses that new technologies are multiplying human information processing capacity by ten every three years. I'll give you his calculation, if you will take it (as scientist Steve Schneider puts it) not literally but seriously: a tenfold increase in efficiency of systems every five years, compounded by an increase in the number of systems by some 30 percent or more a year.

Quite suddenly, human brainwork is the world's dominant skill, and information has become our dominant resource. It will now play the role in economic history that physical labor, stone, bronze, soils, metals, and energy once played.

But information is fundamentally different from all its predecessors as civilization's dominant resource. It's not necessarily depletive, you don't necessarily run out of it; information often expands as it's used. Unlike tangible things or even human bodies, information is readily transportable, at close to the speed of light. Remoteness is fast becoming not a matter of birth or fate, but of choice.

Information leaks so easily, to the chronic astonishment of the White House and the CIA, that it is much harder to hide and to hoard than tangible resources used to be. The spread of education erodes the power that once accrued to the few who were "in the know." Information cannot be owned, though its delivery service can. Giving or selling information is not an exchange transaction; it's a sharing transaction.

The word "communication" comes from the Latin, *communicare*, which doesn't mean to communicate; it means to share. The information environment is a sharing environment. We are going to have to rethink the very basis of copyright and patent law, the distinction between public and private enterprise, and the notion that states "own" what their citizens or officials have discovered.

If the dominant activity of modern civilization is to be the sharing of symbols, rather than the exchange of things, it's high time we created a new framework—a new economics, a new body of law, a new value system, a new kind of politics—that reflects the transformation in the reality around us.

■ ■ ■

What could an "information commons" mean for fairness?

There is an extraordinary recent example of a country called "poor" making wealth by using information to add value. Out of South Korea's experience, Hahn-Been Lee (public administrator, economist, university president, once vice-premier of the Republic of Korea) suggests bold goals for a spreading information commons. He thinks these things could happen within the life expectancy of today's children—"by the year 2020, if not by 2020, then 2050:"

One, universal education: The ability to read and write, and do basic calculations. "Grade school level education in their vernacular languages, in all Indian villages, Chinese villages, Indonesian villages, and African villages may be a bigger order than stopping the global warming."

Two, "available TV sets, color or not, in each household in those millions of villages."

Three, "a telephone in each of those millions of homes."

Lee's order is purposeful, a post-Maslovian hierarchy of values. Most basic of all, he thinks, is the capacity to "learn by letters." Next, not as a substitute for literacy but as reinforcement, comes "the ability to communicate and share images [and] the ability to voice communications." All these are "intellectually and mentally as basic as breathing fresh air and drinking fresh water." Once people-in general get educated, élite behavior will change, not before.

By 2020 or 2050, Lee believes, "the world could be visualized as a sprawling global city where teleconferencing computers can be linked and intellectuals can dialogue worldwide." The "global metropolitan networking" will take care of itself. The informatized elites will insist on being in touch with each other, and the technologies for such linkages will be fully exploited. But the questions are: How do people living in those millions of villages share the benefits of communications? How can the global information commons be operational at the village level?

Part of Lee's answer is to preserve rural life, which has value far beyond its economic productivity. The worst thing would be for small farmers to move in droves to become marginal urban people. If present trends continue, we could see the appalling prospect of cities like Beijing, Shanghai, and Calcutta with 50 million people.

Another part of Lee's answer is to make intergenerational relations easier, more humane. The telephone, and potentially other information technologies, promise to contribute much in maintaining contact between children, parents, and grandparents, wherever in the world they are in an increasingly mobile information commons.

In short, the information commons can contribute to fairness if it is used quite deliberately to empower the powerless and to put them in affective and immediate touch with each other. The key strategy is to make modern information technologies work for small farmers as individuals, as households and—in real-time communication with each other—as value-conscious new stakeholders in a global society.

■ ■ ■

At the Aspen symposium on The Global Commons, we asked two of America's most original thinkers, Shirley Hufstedler and Murray Gell-Mann, to ask themselves what it would do to our conventional wisdoms to consider information—its worldwide flow and our richly diverse cultural heritage—as a "commons." Their responses were so thoughtful that they are reproduced in full in Chapters 11 and 12, as cadenza and coda to this booklet.

11

PRIVATE PROPERTY
IN THE INFORMATION COMMONS

Shirley Hufstedler

When it was proposed in the Constitutional Convention that each session be opened with a prayer, Alexander Hamilton (so a rumor goes) reportedly jumped to his feet with an objection, saying: "I am opposed on principle to calling on any foreign power for help." Few among us are that self-reliant when faced by the need to resolve a paradox rooted in the extraordinary cleverness of the children of Old Adam. The paradox is that the same science and technology which has released millions of human beings from the grinding need to wrench a bare subsistence from the earth has also made it possible for human beings to destroy themselves and the earth as well.

Even with prayers for help from many quarters, foreign and domestic, we have not yet learned how to resolve the many dilemmas posed by science and technology. We have not even shaped an intellectual framework in which to think clearly about how to resolve them.

Medical technology, for instance, has permitted mankind to intervene intimately not only in birth and death, but in the very process of life—a reality that is riddled with complexity. Yet the theological tenets, legal precepts, philosophy of government, and social practices that have earlier been invoked to resolve those issues were developed when only God could intervene. They do not easily retain their conceptual élan under circumstances where mankind has increasingly allocated to itself tasks once left to Divine Providence. Nor in taking on such tasks to ourselves have we been able, alas, simultaneously to endow ourselves with the wisdom attributed to Divinity.

The gap between human cleverness and our capacity to deal with its results extends beyond the province of the health sciences. Technological advances now permit us to transmit and to receive fantastic quantities of data from across the street, around the world, and beyond our solar system. They permit us to hear whispers in the closet and to detect the reverberations of the Big Bang at the birth of the universe. They permit us to store horrendous volumes of data on instrumentalities that are much smaller than a gnat's eyeball and to retrieve them at the will of a computer. They have also created opportunities and problems that exceed our current philosophical grasp—or even the reach of our attention span.

Some people may more favor the ways of Emerson's elderly Boston gentleman who insisted on being awakened every ten minutes from his after-dinner naps to hear the latest news. For my part, however, I sometimes wish that the Information Age was briefly displaced by an Age of Silence during which we could sift through the accumulated masses of data that assail us and find within that detritus an occasional nugget of real, delicious wisdom. My current response to the challenge of information overload is simply to ask my friends what they have read that's worthwhile. I have neither the time, the energy, nor the inclination to dig unaided through the pounds of paper that cross my desk every day, in search of buried treasure.

■ ■ ■

In the old Western world, as elsewhere, power and wealth were defined by the ownership of tangible property and the ability to command labor. For example, English civil law lavishly protected the lands and chattels of the Crown, the Church, and the nobility. Chattels included plows, domestic animals, children, women, and serfs—categories that were not mutually exclusive. Property law was both a reflection and reinforcement of the existing power structure. Control of land and chattels—both were limited resources—was all the property law needed because intangible assets were negligible.

To be sure, information and knowledge have always been things of value, and they are intangible. The small store of those intangibles was then relatively easy to protect by persons who had access to the supply and the strength to make their monopoly prevail. They were primarily members of priestly castes, kings, and warriors—again categories that were not mutually exclusive.

The art of writing was surely the beginning of data storage. As long as only scribes could read and write, information could be controlled by limiting the number of scribes and by restricting those for whom scribes could work. The printing press was the first invention that expanded that resource. Its impact was not felt for many years because knowledge of printing was limited, presses were scarce, and few were literate. It is no accident that from ancient times to the present, those who seek to gain or to maintain power over others rigorously try to prevent access to vital information and knowledge.

The expansion of intangible assets did not happen until clever human beings invented the corporation and created securities markets, financing instruments, and institutions to manage them. More recently, science and technology have together generated multiple revolutions in the growth of the storage, retrieval, and transmission of information and knowledge. Those intangible resources, once scarce, are now abundant, but the old tensions between sharing information for the common good and reserving information and knowledge for private gain are still with us.

Economic, political, and legal theories have not kept abreast of the dizzying pace of technological change. In Western law, for example, property was that which could be reduced to possession. Although exclusive possession was not required, the power to exclude others was thought necessary. With limited exceptions, knowledge and even information are by their nature incapable of exclusive possession. The canons for "mine" and "thine" that we used to invoke in deciding who is entitled to what cannot be readily altered to fit the new technology with the help of a stitch here and a snip there.

Protection of Americans' fundamental liberties is ofttimes stated in the language of tangible property. For instance, the Fourth Amendment to the United States Constitution assures Americans of their right "to be secure in their persons, houses, papers and effects, against unreasonable searches and seizures," and promises that those rights "shall not be violated, and no warrants shall issue, but upon probable cause."

The constitutional draftsmen sought to protect us from the governmental abuses that they knew; they were all too familiar with the Crown's using despised general warrants to justify clumsy physical intrusions into homes and desks. They could not foresee governmental use of invisible searches for intangible things made possible by electronics or the use of other technological miracles of potential mischief to accomplish the incursions they tried to prevent.

Although the draftsmen did not have the powers of Cassandra, those colonial gentlemen did not confine the breadth of their vision simply to mechanics. The values that they were protecting are as important today as they were then: They sought to protect citizens from governmental prying into areas of our individual lives, leaving us the personal privacy that is necessary to human dignity and permitting the government to breach the privacy wall only by showing a neutral magistrate that good cause exists to believe that the person subjected to such indignity has committed a crime.

The vitality of the Fourth Amendment can be preserved despite the new technologies as long as those who interpret the Constitution have the reach of mind to enforce the intangible values of the draftsmen, rather than confining their lofty thoughts to the protection of colonial real estate and chattels.

■ ■ ■

Every society, consciously or not, encourages or discourages the creative potential of its people. The kinds of creativity that are encouraged and in whom they are encouraged have varied widely from society to society and from time to time. In Western Europe during the Middle Ages, for example, the artist who sought to glorify neither the Church nor the Crown was mute.

By contrast, the draftsmen of the United States Constitution sought to encourage many kinds of creativity for the benefit of the whole society. Their premise was that we should be a free people in a free society. They surely knew that education, access to information and knowledge were essential both to encourage creativity and to foster a free society. They also knew that not all Americans were free and that the creativity potential of only a few was cultivated. The knowledge of those facts, however, did not deter them from stating their ideals.

A PLEA FOR PUBLIC EDUCATION
By the Philadelphia Working Man's Committee (1830)

. . . The original element of despotism is a monopoly of talent, which consigns the multitude to comparative ignorance and secures the balance of knowledge on the side of the rich and the rulers. If then the healthy existence of a free government be, as the committee believes, rooted in the will of the American people, it follows as a necessary consequence, of a government based upon that will, that this monopoly should be broken up and that the means of equal knowledge (the only security for equal liberty) should be rendered, by legal provision, the common property of all classes. . . .

When the committees contemplate their own condition and that of the great mass of their fellow laborers, when they look around in the glaring inequality of society, they are constrained to believe that, until the means of equal instruction shall be equally secured to all, liberty is but an unmeaning word, and equality an empty shadow, whose substance to be realized must first be planted by an equal education and proper training in the minds, in the habits, in the manners, and in the feelings of the community.

Even those who wrote that "all men are created equal" had to know that not all ideas are of equal value either to the individual or to the society, that the creative potential of individuals is not equal, and that the resources available to stimulate invention are not unlimited.

The system of values, priorities, and compromises in the realm of intangibles chosen by the draftsmen of the Constitution is illustrated by the First Amendment and by Article I, Section 8. The First Amendment is a grand abstraction: "Congress shall make no law . . . abridging the freedom of speech, or of press. . . ." By contrast, Article I, Section 8, the constitutional foundation for our national system of patents and copyrights, is much more concrete: "The Congress shall have the power . . . to promote the progress of science and useful arts, by securing for limited times to authors and inventors the exclusive right to their respective writings and discoveries."

The First Amendment promises freedom of expression which, as a corollary, implies unfettered dissemination of information and ideas. Article I, Section 8, however, imposes limitations on those "free goods." Therein the founders stated their value judgments about which creators were to be stimulated, what kinds of creations were to be fostered, and how both aims were to be accomplished. Those favored were authors and inventors; the kinds of creations to be stimulated were in the fields of science and useful arts. The incentive was the award of exclusive rights to possession for limited times—an evocation of property law.

The draftsmen's choices were influenced, if not dictated, by the needs of the new land for increased production and by their cultural, philosophic, historical, and legal heritage. The draftsmen left evidence of some of their reasoning; for the rest, we must be content with semi-educated guesses.

History had taught them, as it ought to have taught us, that human beings can be stimulated to produce by fear of retribution or hope for reward. Fear will goad some people some of the time to create, but inventive people are more likely to be influenced by carrots than by sticks. Anticipated rewards in the next life may generate creative incentives in a few, but far more will be stimulated by benefits in this one, and only candidates for canonization will be moved by pure altruism—a reality that escaped the writers of communist dogma.

Perhaps the draftsmen recognized the need for protecting creative people because they are rarely, if ever, welcome in their home towns. As adults or children, they are a pesky nuisance because creativity always challenges the status quo. Everybody seems to have a particular stake in leaving things as they are. Obviously this is true of the powerful people in the society because they have the most to gain by lack of change. Even for the least of us, the status quo can be assuring. It is extremely doubtful that a serf in feudal England ever got ulcers worrying about whether he made the right career choice.

The draftsmen could have chosen rewards that were merely symbolic, but no one then or since has been able to find a reward more universally touching than money. The way to get rich was to create something useful that the creator could exclusively possess. The draftsmen did not seek to reward creators for the purpose of excluding their products from society or of making them wealthy. The intent was to stimulate inventiveness for the benefit of the Nation.

Exclusivity of rights was relatively easy to preserve in colonial times because the methods of reproduction were modest. Explosive technological growth has profoundly changed the capacity for reproduction. When messages were transmitted by wires, cables laid on the ocean floor, or held between book covers, it was fairly simple to distinguish the content of the message from the mechanics of transmission; but when ideas have been reduced to a form that can be read by computers, transmitted by wireless, satellites or lasers, it is increasingly difficult to distinguish the medium from the message or to control either one. Exclusivity of possession is ephemeral when copying can be done without the knowledge, much less the consent, of the holders of the rights.

The appropriate balance between private reward and public good cannot be struck by limiting access to communications technology. Even when it is mechanically or politically possible to destroy access, the results are unacceptable because the effect is to diminish valuable resources that could otherwise supply the needs of millions of human beings—as Mr. Gorbachev has recognized. Shooting fax machines may delay information and temporarily preserve the illusion of control, but at great cost as the current leadership of the People's Republic of China is only beginning to learn.

The remedy is not to discard patent and copyright systems nor otherwise to destroy the incentives for creativity. What is needed is the invention of additional means for protecting the rewards to creators while still disseminating the results for the good of society.

■　■　■

The intangibility of information does not prevent the application of some of the aspects of property in assuring creators of their just rewards. After all, shares of corporate stock, patents, and copyrights are only some of the intangible assets for which we have developed systems of rights of ownership and transfer.

Even though we cannot assure a creator that his right to control a copyrighted work will be exclusive, we can, and in some instances we have, developed reward schemes that are based on the nature and extent of the use. Thus commercial publishers, broadcasters, and film makers constantly arrange advances paid for copyrighted material and even for useful ideas that cannot be copyrighted by estimating anticipated use, i.e., the number of customers who are expected to listen to, to see, or to read the end product. Royalties are usually computed taking into account the actual use of the product by calculating the number of copies sold or the number of people who acknowledged that they have heard or seen a production.

The task of counting actual users when those can number in millions was too daunting to have utility before the era of computers, but today sophisticated sampling techniques coupled with the capacity of computers to store and collate data makes user counting practical.

An interesting example of compensation measured by use is the system developed by the American Society of Composers, Artists, and Publishers ("ASCAP") in dividing the proceeds it receives for its members' works. ASCAP negotiates blanket licenses to radio stations to broadcast the members' compositions. To distribute the proceeds of the licenses fairly, ASCAP records samples from radio stations throughout the United States. Experts listen to the tapes, identify the compositions, and use formulae to compute from the samples the total number of times that each work is reproduced. Distributions are made accordingly.

If use alone were the sole measure of compensation, of course, the composer of a symphony would be grossly undercompensated as compared to a successful writer of pop music. Therefore, ASCAP adjusts the scale of compensation by applying different weights to different kinds of works, bearing in mind not only the number of users, but also its judgments about the quality of the social good derived from the product, the time used for each performance and the time needed by the composer to produce the work.

Analogous systems can probably be developed for other kinds of copyrighted works. Scientific and scholarly books rarely become best sellers. Yet, it cannot be doubted that such works have significant social value and sometimes extraordinary economic value as well. It may be possible to develop a system that would permit compensation to the author based on the quality or value of the work as well as its economic utility.

■　■　■

Technology is rapidly moving us toward a global information network that may transform itself into a global information commons. Nevertheless, we have only begun to think about the means of managing that commons and to develop structures that will enhance rather than diminish the incentives for creativity.

We have a few models to examine that currently exist. Treaties have been successfully negotiated with numerous countries in the world to protect foreign copyrights and patents. Some international associations exist and others can be created to represent different fields of inventive endeavor that could represent their membership in negotiating multilateral contracts and in drafting additional treaties to implement the rapid transfer of ideas while, at the same time, providing incentives to those from whose minds the ideas have sprung.

Harlan Cleveland has been in the forefront of thinking about the new challenges posed by technology and the formation of a global information commons. He has invited all of us to help in searching for the "right" questions, a process that must precede the search for the "right" answers. Harlan is a man whose invitations are hard to resist even by those, like me, whose qualifications for the fray are modest. Some of the questions I might ask are these: What creations are so important for the good of humankind that they should become part of the global commons? Who decides? If rewards are to be given to the creators, what kind of compensation can be fairly devised? Should governments "buy" goods for their own country's commons? If so, should that decision be left to each country and, if not, what kind of international tribunal would be assigned the task and by whose rules?

My purpose in posing these questions is not to suggest that I believe these are the "right" questions. Rather, it is only to stimulate others to enter Harlan's intellectual combat zones. Out of the ensuing debate, we may discover new ways to strike more harmonious balances between private profit and public good.

■ ■ ■

We cannot gainsay the value of developing a global commons of knowledge and information. Of even greater moment, however, is the need to create an ethical commons. Perhaps the former can never be achieved without the development of the latter.

It was a great step forward in human ethics to perceive that "I am my brother's keeper." Today, living on our beautiful and fragile Earth, each of us must realize that he is not only his brother's keeper, but the keeper of his stepsister's children thirteen times removed; those children, in turn, are his keepers whatever the color of their faces, ethnicity, or religion. All of us are the keepers of the planet because each of us and all our progeny are the children of this Earth which makes it possible for any of us to survive.

12

THE PRESERVATION OF CULTURAL DIVERSITY

Murray Gell-Mann

Until the Aspen Symposium, I was not quite sure what the Information Commons was. I tended to think of the commons mostly in terms of the "tragedy of the commons," and I found it hard to visualize the implications of grazing an additional goat on the *Rocky Mountain News.*

However, in this context it is permitted to discuss our common heritage of cultural wisdom, so I shall try to do that. We have dealt here, with biological diversity, including the diversity of ecosystems or biomes, and with the need to avoid destroying, thoughtlessly in a few years, what biological evolution has built over millions of years.

But it is equally relevant to discuss the diversity of human culture. Instead of the gene pool, we deal here with a pool of ideas, knowledge and understanding of nature, monuments and works of art, myths, traditions, institutions, and languages; and we may discuss their conservation. There is more than a superficial parallel with biological diversity. The evolution of organisms, the evolution of ecosystems, the process of individual learning and thinking, the operation of an immune system, and the process of human cultural evolution all have a great deal in common. We call them "complex adaptive systems."

They all collect certain data from their environments, which are evolving too. They use the data for prediction and for actions that will affect survival and the character of future data received. They do all this by encapsulating the learned information in highly compressed packages: models or theories or blueprints—we may refer to them all as schemata. The schemata are subject to change and to competition with one another and their survival depends on their success in prediction and in guiding actions of the complex adaptive systems that generate them.

In biology, the most clear-cut example of a schema is the DNA package carried by each organism. In individual learning, so prominent in human beings, there are the individual schematized theories that each individual organism uses for grasping the reality of the world. In human cultural evolution, which includes the cultural transmission of information, there are myths, traditions, institutions, and especially scientific theories which are, perhaps, the most remarkable examples of compressed information packages with predictive power.

Often scientific theories are not fully in agreement with observation and require modification or replacement by competing theories. In neurotic people, individual schemata can lead to patterns of repeated maladaptive behavior. In the case of the human race, there are traits such as "generalized tribalism"— rampant ethnic hostility, religious bigotry, jingoistic nationalism— that are definitely maladaptive now, even if they were once, perhaps, adaptive in an earlier stage of human development. We are not sure to what extent such traits are genetic and to what extent cultural.

As is well known from biological evolution, mechanisms are typically available for altering these packages: random mutations followed by selection, yielding a search process over a landscape of adaptation. For scientific theories that process works very well. In the case of neuroses, it is notoriously difficult. It is also difficult to affect our communal maladaptive traits. Indeed, the taming of generalized tribalism seems to be one of the hardest, as well as one of the most important, problems facing the human race.

■ ■ ■

But here we are discussing the conservation, not the destruction, of cultural diversity—of those diverse packages of "cultural DNA" that still exist in various parts of the world. When I was a child, I raised with my father the old question of promoting universal peace by using only a single world language. He told me, in reply, how two hundred years ago, in the era of Enlightenment and the French Revolution, the German thinker Herder, a pioneer of the Romantic Movement as well as a figure of the Enlightenment, wrote about the need to preserve linguistic diversity by saving the dying Latvian and Lithuanian languages—so archaic, so close to the original Indo-European. With the aid of native writers of that time, such as the Lithuanian poet Donelaitis, the work of conservation of those bits of cultural DNA was accomplished (as our friend Mikhail Sergeyevich Gorbachev knows so well!).

The most difficult problems of cultural conservation involve tribal peoples, the ones that we sometimes call primitive. Eunice Ribeiro Durham mentioned the present plight of the Yanomamö Indians, on the border of Venezuela and Brazil, the largest indigenous group that has been relatively unaffected by contact with the outside.

Consider the tribal indigenous peoples and their lore and institutions. Think of the knowledge of the properties of plants in the mind of each tribal shaman. Many of those witch doctors are now dying without replacement. The great Harvard ethnobotanist, Richard Schultes, who spent most of his life studying medicinal plants in the Amazon Basin, says that every time a shaman dies, it is as if a library had burned down. Many of those tribal peoples possess precious knowledge of how to live with tropical ecosystems. In general, their ways of life provide a treasure house of information about the possibilities of human organization and modes of thought.

In many cases, these indigenous peoples are being either physically exterminated by disease and violence or else displaced or dispersed and culturally annihilated. A hundred years ago, in my State of California, some people were still shooting wild Indians on weekends. Today, we deplore the same kind of thing in other countries. One hopes that, instead, there can be opportunities for survival and for choice, either to be left more or less alone for the time being or to undergo a somewhat voluntary and organic kind of modernization, with a degree of cultural continuity and with a memory of the past.

■ ■ ■

Note the tension between the universality of the Enlightenment and the need for the preservation of cultural diversity. In discussing the future of the planet, using the results of scientific investigation and attempting to employ rational ways of thinking about the implications of those results, we are hampered by the prevalence of superstition, the persistence of erroneous beliefs. (In Aspen, for example, we are in a center of concentration of weird beliefs!) There is a widespread anachronistic failure to recognize the urgent problems that face humanity on this planet. We are, of course, severely threatened by generalized tribalism in all its many forms, and by philosophical disunity.

Yet we are arguing, at the same time, that cultural diversity is itself a valuable heritage that we must preserve: that Babel of languages, that discord of religious and ethical systems, that panorama of myth, that potpourri of political and social traditions. The same paradox surfaced when Harlan Cleveland remarked that the Global Commons will be governed pluralistically or not at all, with a measure of decentralized control and with varied initiatives bubbling up all over.

He was challenged on the grounds that rational governance requires agreement on principles. He called attention to the same dialectic that we are discussing here, between universalizing factors—science, technology, rationality, education, thinking skills, and human rights—and the particularizing factors such as local culture and beliefs, as well as simple diversity in temperament and occupation and geographical location.

Our discussion makes contact at this point with Shirley Hufstedler's presentation. The information explosion, about which we have heard so much, is really mostly a misinformation explosion. We are exposed to huge amounts of material, data, comments, ideas, conclusions—much of it wrong or misunderstood or just plain confused. There is a crying need for more intelligent commentary and review.

Libraries are technically capable, today, of developing systems that would automatically call up, in any search for papers or documents, each relevant review article, along with an identification of the reviewer that would permit some estimate of his biases. We need to place a higher prestige on that very creative act, the writing of a serious review article, which distinguishes the reliable from the unreliable, which systematizes and encapsulates, in the form of reasonably successful theories and schemata, that which seems reliable.

■　■　■

How, then, in the world of information, do we reconcile the identification and the labeling of error with the tolerance—not only tolerance, but celebration and preservation—of cultural diversity?

Some of us may feel relief rather than sadness at the passing of the Ayatollah Khomeini, but we do not want the idea of an Ayatollah to be completely forgotten. (We should recall, by the way, in connection with modern information technology, the role of audio cassettes in his coming to power.)

When Bishop Landa burned nearly all of the books of the Maya in the Yucatán in the sixteenth century, he probably knew that he was wiping out a large fraction of the Yucatec Maya cultural heritage. But he thought, also, that there was an association of some kind between those books and the rites that he so deplored many of which we secular observers of today would probably consider barbaric as well.

Even the Roman Catholic Church learned some lessons in this domain; the methods of conversion changed over time. In New Mexico, after the Pueblo Revolt of 1680 and Spanish reconquest of 1692, the Church no longer attempted to eradicate so many of the Pueblo ceremonial customs and institutions, but tried to build on them, to alter them gradually. Today, Archbishop Sanchez of Santa Fe does not object to deer dances at the Pueblos, even in the churches on Christmas Eve.

Perhaps our universalizing and secular culture, with its emphasis on science, thinking skills, education with freedom of thought, the rights of the human individual can react in a somewhat analogous way to the other patterns of thought and behavior on the planet, even those that are associated with cruel harassment and persecution of that very scientific and secular culture.

91

We can try to persuade the adherents of those patterns to be less fanatical, more flexible about their systems of thought, and at first to tolerate, and later grudgingly to accept many of our universal ideas—while incorporating into the universal culture detailed knowledge about more parochial systems, myths, customs, and institutions, along with attempts to understand both their appeal and their function.

We need also a respectful appreciation of the discoveries that have been made in the development of those systems, whether ethnobotanical discoveries, discoveries in the realm of mystical experience, discoveries about the possibilities of human nature, or discoveries about how to live in rough equilibrium with a tropical environment. Of particular importance may be discoveries about how to restrain the appetite for material goods and substitute more spiritual appetites.

The course of modernization has not usually been this ethnologically sensitive; and the violence of the reaction, as in contemporary Iran, should tell us something important—just as the Franciscan Fathers finally learned from the Pueblo Revolt.

In the long run, of course, it may require much more than sensitivity. It may require very profound new developments in the behavioral sciences if we are to learn how to modify for the human race, as a whole, maladaptive traits like generalized tribalism and abuse of the environment, while preserving both individual freedom and cultural diversity. The cure of individual neuroses is not easy; the same is true of social neuroses. But some of our current slogans will be helpful—"Unity in Diversity," "Think Globally, Act Locally," and our national slogan, "E Pluribus Unum."

AFTERWORD

60 Propositions
About The Global Commons

There is no way to capture in a few simple aphorisms the prodigious complexity of the Global Commons. But it may be useful to collect in one place some key facts and ideas, some striking metaphors, some elements of a gathering policy consensus.

These 60 propositions are not an "executive summary." But they are derived from the 12 chapters of this booklet, and organized accordingly. They are many people's ideas, unattributed here and without the quotation marks that are found in the foregoing text. Taken together, I believe they constitute a direction-finder for a new policy frontier

1. Concept of the Commons

■ Four enormous physical environments, still mostly unexplored, are treated in international law and custom as parts of a global commons. Outer space, the atmosphere, the oceans, and Antarctica are geophysically and biochemically related to one another—and cousins also in the human psyche. It should be useful to think about our surround as if its parts were related to each other. Because they are.

■ The Commons environments as such belong to no one—or to everyone at once. What isn't owned exclusively cannot be bought, sold, given or seized. It has to be shared.

2. Awareness of the Commons

■ Some time in recent years, the works of human beings began to outweigh the works of nature in the global scheme of things. Humankind has become a more important agent of environmental change than nature.

■ In our time there is a new class of problems, requiring unprecedented kinds of solutions. They are global: people everywhere have to widen the scale of what they worry about. And they are behavioral: the pace and direction of global change can only be modified by what we (humanity) do, or stop doing, next.

■ An ecumenical movement in the biological and earth sciences is bringing together disciplines that have been focusing separately on the atmosphere, the oceans, agriculture, forestry, geology, geophysics, and outer space. The governance of the Global Commons is to the social sciences what "global change" is to the natural sciences. In a word, it's the next frontier.

3. Metaphors in the Commons

■ The new fraternity of space explorers spoke not of nations, of continents, of islands, but of our earth, our planet, our world. They neglected to mention its divisions, but found it whole and blue and beautiful.

■ This shift of perspective had nothing to do with the physical reality of our planet and the universe of which it is so small and precious a part. The physical world was there right along. The difference now is that we have realized our own impact on our surroundings—and that in consequence we are changing our minds, creating new metaphors by which to guide our actions together.

■ For example: We will only discover and develop the ocean's potentials if we abandon old metaphors—lurking perils, stormy weather, dangerous depths, the wrath of Medusa, a

94

place of death—that are out of touch with modern marine technology.

■ As another example: the prospect of global warming is not well conveyed by the image of a "greenhouse," a pleasant place full of pretty flowers. What's ahead is something more like a "heat trap."

4. Fairness in the Commons

■ The costs and benefits of actions to protect and develop the atmospheric commons will have to be shared in a manner widely agreed to be "fair." Otherwise the commons will come to be just another arena for bitter and continuous conflict.

■ The poor and the rich, we are cooperating to destroy the environment in different ways. The destruction that leads the poor to deepen their own poverty is the same process which leads to consumption by the rich, that pollutes the environment from which the resources are taken.

5. The Commons as a System

■ The real commons is not a place or a space but a system.

■ If the Global Commons is a system, we have to establish "boundary conditions" that enable us to sustain it. Once boundary conditions are widely understood, there is plenty of room for a pluralism of choices by many different kinds of organizations—private, nonprofit, public—to stay inside the agreed limits.

■ The threat of climate change gives us a whole new set of incentives to do what we ought to be doing anyway, like replanting forests and regreening deserts.

■ Brotherhood, caring, working together are no longer simply pious ideals divorced from the realities of life, but the indispensable ingredients of human survival.

95

6. Diversity in the Commons

■ The essence of our "common heritage" is biological diversity, the basic library of life on Earth.

■ Individual species represent accumulated experience over evolutionary time, solutions to unique sets of biological problems, embodying important information about what works and what doesn't work.

■ Biological diversity is our most sensitive environmental litmus paper. If an area (say, a river valley) maintains its biological diversity over time, that's the very definition of "sustainable use."

■ Biodiversity is not just another environmental problem. We are plagued with acid rain, oil spills, and the results of urban congestion—vehicle pollution, traffic jams, sewage and garbage disposal. Trends such as these are reversible sooner or later. But the loss of biological diversity is forever.

■ Treating local forests as global treasures gives promise of joint efforts to save national resources of global value. The idea of swapping "debt for nature" may play a role here. But first we have to learn to convert international debt from a "problem" into an opportunity.

■ We can't make a Xerox copy of the biosphere, and leave this one behind as a degraded toxic waste dump. You can't negotiate with the environment.

7. Alarm and Uncertainty in the Commons

■ There is already a striking consensus among scientists that if present trends continue our globe is going to get warmer—perhaps by an average of 6 degrees Celsius (much more at the poles, much less at the Equator). We are not accustomed to thinking ahead a hundred years, yet that is within the lifetimes of some children already born.

96

■ The "forcing functions" (the physical and chemical reactions that are bound to change our future climate, and the effects they produce) are real, they are sustained, they are growing, and they are directly related to human activities. There is no magic thermostat to stabilize the earth.

■ In the last Ice Age it was only 5 to 9 degrees (Celsius) colder, on average, than it is today. The transition time may have been as much as 10,000 years—which translates as a change of 1 or 2 degrees every thousand years, as a measure of "natural" change. With the "greenhouse effect," we're looking at an increase of 2 to 8 degrees in a hundred years. That's 10 to 40 times the "natural" rate of change. So we are facing global climate change without precedent.

■ Nobody experiences "global change"; all the important changes are regional. In the coastal zones, the face of climate change will be erosion, and the intrusion of salt water. In the mid-latitudes, the problems will be with forests rather than crops. In the higher latitudes, there will be dramatic effects on agriculture, transportation, resource development, and military deployments. (If there's less ice pack, there's less room to hide submarines.)

■ We need to develop our resilience, our capacity to adapt to conditions without precedent, in order to deal with climate and other environmental changes that are already in the cards.

8. Policy for the Commons

■ In the Global Commons the scientific uncertainties are the easy part. The rest of it, the policy part, is the biggest challenge that ever faced civilization.

■ Climate change integrates our thinking about the Global Commons. If the Commons is the Earth system itself, climate and climate change are the central environmental issue to which all the stakeholders (that is, all of us) will have to address themselves.

■ For global warming a viable "boundary condition" might be a global ceiling for emissions, through human activities, of "greenhouse gases." Such a target might be to stop well short of a doubling of pre-industrial levels of greenhouse gases in the global atmosphere. That would mean something like a 20% increase in their concentration compared with what it is now.

■ Emissions by the United States are roughly 25% of the problem. U.S. actions, to help meet such a global goal, would include much better fuel efficiency (cars that get much more than the present standard of 27.5 miles to the gallon); moving away from coal and oil toward natural gas; a new look at nuclear energy, this time taking safety, waste and proliferation fully into account; a new push on solar energy, including energy from the difference between deep cold and warm surface ocean water. Also on the "must" list: improving water efficiency; coastal zone management in anticipation of a rise in sea levels; genetic engineering of plants to use less water and fewer chemicals; the cutoff of chlorofluoro-carbons (CFCs) and their replacement by safer alternatives; preservation and enhancement of forests; helping reduce population growth around the world; and technology-sharing to a degree that would mean a new dimension in international cooperation.

■ The costs of change are worrisome. Public regulations should be used sparingly, because the half-life of regulatory rigidities is long (25 to 50 years). But humans are not just economic beings; as information leaks around the world, people take notice and make big policy changes possible.

■ Abating global warming may even come to be regarded not as dangerously costly, but as very profitable. To the extent that it can be profitable, it should be done not through mandatory regulation but through the market. The real danger is that we will "fiddle while coal burns."

■ The bottom line is what people—millions of people—will be willing to do, or stop doing. So the essence of global/

behavioral change is the pervasive spread of knowledge. People-in-general have to get the idea before the policy announcers (intellectuals, politicians, government officials, corporate executives, community leaders) can summon the courage to "make policy."

9. Cohesion and Consensus on the Commons

■ The concept of a Global Commons is a fresh—because more inclusive—framework for thinking about our total environment.

■ We are beyond the point of needing more research before acting. There are, of course, great benefits in more research to reduce uncertainties and refine strategies. But we need to act on what we know.

■ Nongovernment approaches and pluralistic mechanisms will be front and center in managing global change.

■ Education about the Global Commons, from kindergarten to adult learning, should be aimed at patterns of behavior and value systems consistent with a sharing environment. The media, political leadership, and nongovernments all have a role to play in pushing education compatible with the concept of the Commons.

■ Should we impose our values on still-vacant environments? How could we do otherwise? If we don't impose values such as environmental prudence, protection of diversity, and a balance of human rights and responsibilities, then we will make the Commons a new arena for old-fashioned wars fought with new-fangled weapons.

■ The management of the Commons requires a two-tier system: public authorities developing consensus on standards, norms, goals, and codes of ethics; and many different enterprises and authorities—the private sector doing most of the job—acting within the agreed standards/norms, *without* the need for detailed international decision-making or heavy international bureaucracies.

■ The Montreal Protocol restraining the use of ozone-eating CFCs is an interesting model, if a controversial one. It worked because there was an international scientific consensus on what was wrong and what to do about it; information flowed freely between leaders and wider publics; the factfinding process was innovative, folding in people from many walks of life; there was an active international facilitator (UNEP, the U.N. Environment Programme); and the treaty set targets but left to the market the task of reducing CFCs. For reasons of fairness, the emissions targets were tougher on the industrial countries than on developing countries. And those targets were left open, for further revision later on, in a flexible and dynamic process.

■ It will be important to resist the temptation to change people's behavior by coercion once leaders decide that behavioral change is essential. Can we avoid autocratic solutions in reacting to potential catastrophe? The answer has to be yes: it's not enough to survive, we have to survive in freedom.

■ The world is inching its way toward a new consensus. The environment is fast moving to the top of the world's agenda. Beyond "human rights" there is human solidarity, a fairly new idea that transcends national boundaries and may turn out to be the glue that holds us all together.

10. The Brainwork Commons

■ It was the fusion of computers and telecommunications that made possible an environmental perspective and brought to the fore the idea of a Global Commons. But there is another kind of commons. The accumulated lore of civilized humanity, not only "recorded history" but the know-what of scientific inquiry, the know-how of technology, the

100

know-why of values and the know-who of social institutions—not to mention our hunches from unremembered subconscious learnings—are certainly part of the "common heritage" of humankind.

■ The spread of knowledge, encouraging people by the millions to think for themselves, has produced a worldwide demand for choice, for participation, for "democracy."

■ Information technologies—mass media such as television but also person-to-person devices such as facsimile—have helped make human brainwork the world's dominant skill, knowledge the world's dominant resource, and the sharing of symbols (rather than the exchange of things) the dominant activity of modern civilization.

■ The idea of information as a commons—if enough people take it seriously—could be good news for fairness. It would require giving the highest priority to universal education (the ability to read and write and do basic calculations), and spreading TV sets and telephones to every rural village. The education of the masses changes the behavior of elites, as they respond to the formerly powerless, empowered by information technologies to be value-conscious stakeholders in a global society.

11. Private Property in the Information Commons

■ The gap between human cleverness and our capacity to deal with it is illustrated by the trouble we have got into, trying to apply long-developed notions about the ownership of tangible property in an information economy where intangible resources are increasingly dominant.

■ Economic, political and legal theories have not kept abreast of the dizzying pace of technological change. Now that intangible resources are abundant—not held by an educated few and denied to the uneducated many—the old tensions between sharing information for the common good and reserving information and knowledge for private gain have been intensified.

■ The vitality of the Fourth Amendment can be preserved despite the new technologies as long as those who interpret the Constitution have the reach of mind to enforce the intangible values of the draftsmen, rather than confining their lofty thoughts to the protection of colonial chattels and real estate.

■ Even those who wrote that "all men are created equal" had to know that not all ideas are of equal value either to the individual or to the society, that the creative potential of individuals is not equal, and that the resources to stimulate invention are not unlimited.

■ Fear will goad some people some of the time to create, but inventive people are more likely to be influenced by carrots than by sticks. The Constitutional draftsmen did not seek to reward creators for the purpose of excluding their products from society or of making them wealthy. The intent was to stimulate inventiveness for the benefit of the Nation.

■ The appropriate balance between private reward and public good cannot be struck by limiting access to communications technology. Shooting fax machines may delay information and temporarily preserve the illusion of control, but at great cost— as the current leadership of the People's Republic of China is only beginning to learn.

■ Technology is rapidly moving us toward a global information commons. But we have only begun to think about how to manage the commons so as to enhance rather than diminish the incentives for creativity. Some of the relevant questions for this rethinking are these: What creations are so important for the good of humankind that they should become part of the global commons? If rewards are to be given to the creators, what kind of compensation can be fairly devised? And who decides?

12. The Preservation of Cultural Diversity

■ Biological diversity is important. But equally relevant is the diversity of human culture. Instead of the gene pool, we deal here with a pool of ideas, knowledge and understanding of nature, monuments and works of art, myths, traditions, institutions, and languages.

■ There is more than a superficial parallel with biological diversity. The evolution of organisms and ecosystems, the processes of individual learning and thinking, the operation of an immune system, and the process of human cultural evolution all have a great deal in common. We call them "complex adaptive systems."

■ In neurotic people, there is repeated maladaptive behavior. In the human race there is "generalized tribalism"—rampant ethnic hostility, religious bigotry, jingoistic nationalism—that is definitely maladaptive now, even if once, perhaps, adaptive in an earlier stage of human development. The taming of generalized tribalism seems to be one of the hardest, as well as one of the most important, problems facing the human race.

■ We have to worry about the loss of "cultural DNA" as traditional peoples die of civilized diseases or are culturally annihilated. When some tribal shamans die without replacement, it is as if a library had burned down. Many tribal peoples possess precious knowledge of how to live with tropical ecosystems; their ways of life provide a treasure house of information about the possibilities of human organization and modes of thought.

■ Cultural diversity is itself a valuable heritage that we must preserve: that Babel of languages, that discord of religious and ethical systems, that panorama of myth, that potpourri of political and social traditions.

■ The information explosion is also, perhaps mostly, a misinformation explosion. We are exposed to huge amounts of

103

materials, data, comments, ideas, conclusions—much of it wrong or misunderstood or just plain confused. There is a crying need for more intelligent commentary and review—for that very creative act, the writing of a serious review article which systematizes and encapsulates and distinguishes the reliable from the unreliable.

■ We can try to persuade the adherents of fanatical patterns of thought to be more tolerant of universal ideas such as the Global Commons. But at the same time we should try to incorporate into the universal culture more informed and sympathetic knowledge of the more parochial systems, myths, customs and institutions, trying hard to understand their appeal and their function. The cure of individual neuroses is not easy; the same is true of social neuroses.

PARTICIPANTS IN
THE ASPEN INSTITUTE SYMPOSIUM
ON THE GLOBAL COMMONS

Robert O. Anderson

A native of Chicago and a graduate of the University of Chicago, Mr. Anderson is a petroleum executive, rancher, and civic leader. In 1963, he was elected to the Board of Directors of Atlantic Richfield Company (ARCO) and later served as both Chief Executive Officer and Chairman of the Board for a period of 17 years. He is now President and CEO of Hondo Oil & Gas Company and CEO of Pauley Petroleum, Inc. Over the past 50 years his business endeavors have included exploration, production, refining and marketing of oil, as well as cattle raising, mining, and general manufacturing. Mr. Anderson's interests extend into the political arena. He has served as a member of the Republican National Committee. He is Honorary Chairman of The Aspen Institute and serves in many public and charitable organizations.

Richard Elliot Benedick

Mr. Benedick is currently a Senior Fellow of the World Wildlife Fund and The Conservation Foundation. He is on detail from the State Department, where he was Deputy Assistant Secretary for environment, health, and natural resource issues and chief U.S. negotiator for the Montreal Protocol on protection of the ozone layer. He had previously served as Coordinator of Population Affairs (with rank of ambassador) and has held diplomatic posts in Athens, Bonn, Paris, Karachi, and Tehran. Mr. Benedick has headed U.S. delegations to numerous international meetings, and has published and lectured here and abroad on economics, environment, population, and development. A *summa cum laude*

105

graduate of Columbia, he has an M.A. in economics from Yale, a Ph.D. from the Harvard Graduate School of Business Administration, and was Evans Fellow in metaphysical poetry at Oxford.

Noel J. Brown

A citizen of Jamaica, Mr. Brown is Special Representative of the Executive Director and Regional Director of the United Nations Environment Programme in North America, based at United Nations headquarters in New York City. He previously served as Political Affairs Officer in the Department of Political and Security Council Affairs at the United Nations. Dr. Brown has also been Visiting Professor on International Law and Organization and Government and Politics at the University of the West Indies, City University, New York, and Distinguished Lecturer at the University of Victoria in British Columbia. He received his M.A. degree in International Law and Organization at Georgetown and his Ph.D. in International Law and Relations from Yale University.

Ralph J. Cicerone

As Director and Senior Scientist in the Atmospheric Chemistry Division of the National Center for Atmospheric Research in Boulder, Colorado, Dr. Cicerone's work includes research on atmospheric chemicals, such as methane and chlorofluorocarbons, that contribute to the greenhouse effect and ozone layer destruction—their origins, their behavior in the atmosphere and their rates of change—and the human activities that emit such gases. Dr. Cicerone received his B.S. degree in electrical engineering from the Massachusetts Institute of Technology and his M.S. and Ph.D. degrees from the University of Illinois, where he studied electrical engineering and physics. He serves on many committees of federal agencies and the National Research Council/National Academy of Sciences.

William C. Clark

Since 1987, Dr. Clark has been a faculty member of the Science, Technology, and Public Policy Program of the John F. Kennedy School of Government at Harvard University. His research focuses on policy issues arising through the interactions of national and international concerns for environment, development, and security. He is currently working on the development of fair assessment frameworks for use in the management of climate change and on the comparative performance of national efforts to deal with global environment-economy interactions. Previously, Dr. Clark led the team of scholars from eastern and western countries conducting the Program on Sustainable Development of the Biosphere at the International Institute for Applied Systems Analysis in Austria. He is a member of the U.S. National Academy of Sciences' Committee for Global Change and coeditor of *Environment*—a monthly magazine of international environment affairs. He received his bachelor's degree in biology from Yale University and a Ph.D. in zoology from the University of British Columbia.

Harlan Cleveland

Mr. Cleveland, political scientist and public executive, was the first dean, and is now professor emeritus, of the University of Minnesota's Hubert H. Humphrey Institute of Public Affairs. He has been a Rhodes Scholar, a U.N. relief administrator, a Marshall Plan executive, a magazine editor and publisher, graduate school dean, Assistant Secretary of State for International Organization Affairs, U.S. Ambassador to NATO, and President of the University of Hawaii. From 1974 to 1980 he was director of The Aspen Institute's Program in International Affairs; he was recently appointed a Distinguished Fellow of the Institute. He is a past president of the American Society for Public Administration, and a Fellow of the World Academy of Art and Science. He currently directs a four-year international project, "Rethinking International Governance," which includes an exploration of the Global Commons concept. His most recent book is *The Knowledge Executive: Leadership in an Information Society*.

John P. Craven

Since 1977, Dr. Craven has been Director of the Law of the Sea Institute at the University of Hawaii and Professor of Law at the affiliated William S. Richardson School of Law. A quartermaster aboard the battleship *New Mexico*, he subsequently received civil engineering degrees from Cornell University and the California In-

107

stitute of Technology. As a senior scientist in the U.S. Navy, he had major responsibilities for the development of the *Polaris* submarines and missiles and was subsequently involved with the development of *Sealabs* II and III, the nuclear-powered research submarine NR-1, the Deep Submergence Rescue Vehicle, and submarine equipage for special undersea missions. Dr. Craven was also chief technical advisor for the searches for the hydrogen bomb lost off Palomares, Spain, and the nuclear attack submarine *Scorpion*. Dr. Craven was a member of the State Department Advisory Committee on the Law of the Sea (1970–83) and has organized a new entity, the Common Heritage Corporation, the mission of which is to implement modern ocean technology and science in the Pacific region.

Eunice Ribeiro Durham

Dr. Durham is a Professor of Social Anthropology and Political Science at the University of São Paolo in Brazil. Formerly, she served as President of the Brazilian Association of Anthropology and continues to hold the position of Vice President of the Brazilian Society for the Advancement of Science. Professor Durham is also a member of the Brazilian Commission of Scientific Associations. Her research centers on social and political movements and she has published many articles and books on related subjects.

Darius W. Gaskins, Jr.

Dr. Gaskins has been President and Chief Executive Officer of Burlington Northern Railroad since 1985. He began his career as a Captain in the U.S. Air Force and later taught industrial organization, econometrics, and microeconomic theory at the University of California, Berkeley. In 1973 he became Assistant Director for Economics at the Office of Policy Analysis in the Department of the Interior, and he subsequently served in the Federal Trade Commission, the Civil Aeronautics Board, the Department of Energy, and the Interstate Commerce Commission. He joined Burlington Northern in 1982. A graduate of the United States Military Academy, Dr. Gaskins received two M.S.E. degrees in Astronautical Engineering and Instrumentation Engineering and a Ph.D. in Economics from the University of Michigan, and has published numerous articles and essays on related topics.

Murray Gell-Mann

Dr. Gell-Mann, the Robert A. Millikan Professor of Physics at the California Institute of Technology since 1967, was recipient of the 1969 Nobel Prize in Physics for his work on the theory of elementary particles. He has been a member of the California Institute of Technology faculty since 1955. In 1952 he discovered the quantity called "strangeness." In 1961 he suggested the "eightfold way" classification scheme, and later proposed quarks and colored gluons as the fundamental constituents of strongly interacting particles such as the neutron and proton. A graduate of Yale with a Ph.D. from MIT, Dr. Gell-Mann is a Citizen Regent of the Smithsonian Institution and Chairman of the Board of the Aspen Center for Physics. Although a theoretical physicist, his interests extend to many other subjects, including natural history, historical linguistics, archaeology, history, depth psychology, and creative learning and thinking. His recent research has focused on complex adaptive systems, which bring together all these areas of study. His policy concerns reach into world environmental quality, restraint in population growth, sustainable economic development, and world political stability including strategic arms control.

Shirley Mount Hufstedler

A graduate of Stanford University Law School, Mrs. Hufstedler practiced law in Los Angeles during the 1950s and later served as Special Legal Consultant to the Attorney General of California in the Colorado River litigation before the U.S. Supreme Court. In 1961, she was appointed Judge of the Los Angeles County Superior Court and was elected to the position in 1962. Under President Lyndon B. Johnson, she was appointed Judge of the United States Court of Appeals for the Ninth Circuit, retaining that position for eleven years until President Jimmy Carter appointed her Secretary of Education. Currently, in addition to being a partner in Hufstedler, Miller, Kaus & Beardsley in Los Angeles, Mrs. Hufstedler serves on the Board of Directors of several prominent corporations. She is also a member of the Board of Trustees for The Aspen Institute, the Carnegie Endowment for International Peace, the California Institute of Technology, the National Policy Exchange, the Institute for Judicial Administration, Occidental College, and the Salzburg

Seminar. Mrs. Hufstedler is an enthusiastic grandmother, gardener, cook, and mountaineer.

Thomas E. Lovejoy

Dr. Lovejoy has been Assistant Secretary for External Affairs of the Smithsonian Institution since 1987. He is a tropical and conservation biologist and has worked in the Amazon region of Brazil for more than 20 years. From 1973 to 1987 he directed the program of the World Wildlife Fund–U.S., serving as the Fund's Executive Vice President from 1985 to 1987. He was the founder of the popular public television series *Nature*, serving as the program's principal advisor for many years. In the field of international conservation he is the originator of the concept of international debt for nature swaps—three programs are already underway in Bolivia, Costa Rica, and Ecuador. Currently, he is chairman of the U.S. Man and Biosphere Program and a member of the Executive Committee of SCOPE (Scientific Committee on Problems of the Environment); he was recently appointed to the White House Science Council as its first environmental scientist.

Amory B. Lovins

Mr. Lovins is the cofounder (in 1982), Director of Research and CFO of the Rocky Mountain Institute, an independent nonprofit foundation which fosters resource efficiency and global security. He has been active in energy policy in some 20 countries over as many years. For the past decade, Mr. Lovins has worked as a team with his wife and colleague Hunter, a lawyer, sociologist, political scientist, and forester. Their work has focused on finding alternative solutions to energy problems, and is especially noted for the "end-use/least-cost" redefinition of the energy problem. In addition to advising numerous utilities and other corporations and public and international agencies, the Lovinses have published a dozen books and several hundred papers. Mr. Lovins, formerly a consultant experimental physicist, was educated at Harvard and Oxford, has held various academic chairs and served on the Department of Energy's senior advisory board. He has received the Onassis Foundation's Delphi Prize and (jointly with Mrs. Lovins) a Mitchell Prize and a Right Livelihood Award.

William A. Nitze

At the time of the Aspen symposium, Mr. Nitze was Deputy Assistant Secretary of State for Environment, Health, and Natural Resources. He was responsible for policy formulation and international negotiations on such issues as acid rain, global climate, regional seas protection, biotechnology, hazardous substances, ozone layer protection, the international AIDS pandemic, and tropical forest and wildlife conservation. Mr. Nitze was previously assistant general counsel, Exploration and Producing Division, at Mobil Oil Corporation in New York. He holds B.A.s from Harvard and Oxford, and a J.D. from Harvard Law School. Mr. Nitze is a trustee of The Aspen Institute and a member of the Advisory Council for the School of Advanced International Studies, Johns Hopkins University.

Jose Pedro de Oliveira-Costa

A native of São Paolo, Brazil, Mr. Oliveira-Costa is the elected Regional Counselor of the International Union for the Conservation of Nature, and was most recently elected as Coordinator of the Atlantic Forest Consortium for five states in Brazil. With a Ph.D. in Environmental Structures from the University of São Paolo, a graduate degree in Architecture and Urban Design from MacKenzie University, São Paolo, and a masters in Environmental Planning from the University of California, Berkeley, he has been active in Brazilian environmental affairs for the past decade. He was responsible for several environmental preservation projects, including those of five major forests, organizer and first executive secretary of the State of São Paolo Environmental Council, consultant and organizer of the Latin American meeting of the Brundtland Commission, and the first State Environment Secretary for the State of São Paolo.

Walter Orr Roberts

Dr. Roberts is President Emeritus of the University Corporation for Atmospheric Research (UCAR), Research Associate of the National Center for Atmospheric Research (NCAR), and Senior Fellow of The Aspen Institute. In 1940, Dr. Roberts began the operation of the High Altitude Observatory in Colorado to photograph the sun's prominences and corona by means of a newly invented solar telescope, the "coronagraph," of which he completed the Western Hemisphere's first example. Over the years, the observatory evolved into what now comprises the research division of NCAR. Dr. Roberts was the first director of NCAR from 1960–73. Dr. Roberts is a graduate of Amherst College and received his M.A. and Ph.D. degrees from Harvard University in Solar Astrophysics.

Claudine Schneider

Ms. Schneider is the Republican Member of Congress for Rhode Island's second district. She was first elected to Congress in 1980 and has been reelected four times. She is a senior Republican on several key environmental subcommittees and has championed a wide range of legislation to protect the environment, to preserve endangered species, and to promote a balanced use of natural resources. In the 100th Congress, the President signed into law her legislation calling for a global effort to prevent the extinction of plants and animals through an International Convention on Biological Diversity. She has also been a leader in a successful promotion to stop ocean pollution from deep-sea dumping of sludge and to stiffen the penalties for medical waste dumping in the ocean. Ms. Schneider worked for the passage of the Wolpe-Schneider Hazardous Waste Reduction Act, a bill promoting technology to reduce the generation of hazardous waste at the source. She cofounded and is the cochair of the Congressional Competitiveness Caucus.

Stephen H. Schneider

Dr. Schneider is currently Head of the Interdisciplinary Climate Systems Section at the National Center for Atmospheric Research. His current research interests include climatic change, food/climate issues, environmental policy, and climatic modeling of paleoclimates and human impact on climate. He is author of *The Genesis Strategy: Climate and Global Survival* (with L. Mesirow), 1976, and *The Coevolution of Climate and Life* (with R. Londer), 1984. His most recent book is *Global Warming*, published in 1989. Dr. Schneider has contributed to *NOVA, Planet Earth, 20/20,* and numerous other television programs in several countries and was selected by *Science Digest* in December 1984 as one of the "One Hundred Outstanding Young Scientists in America." A Fellow of the American Association for the Advancement of Science, he holds a Ph.D. in Mechanical Engineering and Plasma Physics from Columbia University.

Soedjatmoko

Soedjatmoko, who died in December 1989 at the age of 68, was born in Sumatra and began his career in the foreign press department of Indonesia's Ministry of Information. After spending several years as an editor, he served on Indonesia's delegation to the United Nations. He was a member of the Indonesian Constituent Assembly (1956–59), ambassador to the United States (1968–71) and special adviser on social and cultural affairs to the chairman of the National Development Planning Agency (1971–80). He was rector of the U.N. University in Tokyo from 1980 to 1988. Soedjatmoko had written extensively on international affairs and development issues. He was a former trustee of The Aspen Institute and of the Ford Foundation.

Maurice F. Strong

Mr. Strong is a native of Manitoba, Canada. He is the current Chairman of Strovest Holdings, Inc. in Canada; Chairman of American Water Development, Inc. in Denver; and Chairman of the Council, World Economic Forum in Geneva. He is also President of the World Federation of United Nations Associations in Geneva, and a member of the International Advisory Board of Unisys Corporation. A Canadian businessman for much of his career, Mr. Strong has also served as head of Canada's International Development Assistance Program, Secretary General of the U.N. Conference on the Human Environment (1970–72) and Executive Director of the U.N. Environment Programme (1973–75).

Robert M. White

Dr. White is the President of the National Academy of Engineering in Washington, DC, and former president of the University Corporation for Atmospheric Research (UCAR) in

113

Boulder, Colorado. He started his career as a scientist in the Air Force Cambridge Research Center. From 1963 to 1977 he served in the Department of Commerce and was Administrator of the National Oceanographic and Atmospheric Administration (NOAA) from 1970 to 1977. He is a member of the U.S.–Brazil Presidential Committee on Science and Technology, the Advisory Committee for the Kennedy School of Government Program Council for Minorities in Engineering. He also serves on the board of Resources for the Future. He graduated from Harvard University and completed his postgraduate work at MIT.

Timothy E. Wirth

Mr. Wirth was elected to the United States Senate in November 1986, and is the 30th Senator to represent Colorado. He specializes in the fields of the environment, conventional arms control, budget policy, and financial institutions and is a member of four related Senate committees. He is the author of the major Senate legislation addressing the issue of global warming and has also been a leading spokesman for stronger federal clean air laws. He pays special attention to Colorado's conservation, public health, and environment. The Wirth family has been in Colorado for five generations. Mr. Wirth received his B.A. and M.A. degrees from Harvard and a Ph.D. from Stanford. He is an avid outdoorsman.

INDEX

CASSANDRA   Reflections in a Mirror